William J. Kirkpatrick

Unfading Treasures

a compilation of sacred songs and hymns

William J. Kirkpatrick

Unfading Treasures
a compilation of sacred songs and hymns

ISBN/EAN: 9783337089788

Printed in Europe, USA, Canada, Australia, Japan

Cover: Foto ©Lupo / pixelio.de

More available books at **www.hansebooks.com**

Unfading Treasures:

A COMPILATION OF

Sacred Songs and Hymns,

ADAPTED FOR USE BY

SUNDAY-SCHOOLS,
EPWORTH LEAGUES, ENDEAVOR SOCIETIES,
PASTORS,
EVANGELISTS, CHORISTERS, Etc.

EDITORS:

W. J. KIRKPATRICK, JNO. R. SWENEY,
AND T. C. O'KANE.

CINCINNATI:
CRANSTON & CURTS,
Chicago and St. Louis.

PHILADELPHIA:
JOHN J. HOOD,
1024 Arch Street.

Copyright, 1893, by John J. Hood, and Cranston & Curts.

Price, board covers, 35 cents per copy, mailed; $3.60 per dozen, at store.

COPYRIGHT, 1893, BY JOHN J. HOOD, AND CRANSTON & CURTS.

PREFACE.

In the vast field of Sacred Song, to which numerous additions are annually made, of a truth it may be said, "Many are called, but few chosen." While the vast majority of these hymns and tunes either fall flat entirely, or have at the best but a brief existence, yet occasionally there are some which seem to be born with something of immortality in them, and they become what we may appropriately designate as "UNFADING TREASURES."

Many of these have come down to us through the hallowed days of the past, while others, though of more modern origin and inspiration, yet possess the same spirit that "brightened Isaiah's vivid page."

From the former, and the latter, through the kindness of authors, publishers, and other owners of copyrights, the compilers have made this collection of Sacred Songs, which, we trust, will enable all who use it to "sing with the spirit and with the understanding also."

JNO. R. SWENEY.
WM. J. KIRKPATRICK.
T. C. O'KANE.

COPYRIGHT NOTICE.

To PRINT, for sale or otherwise, any copyright hymn of this collection, unless written permission shall have been obtained, is an infringement of copyright.   THE PUBLISHERS.

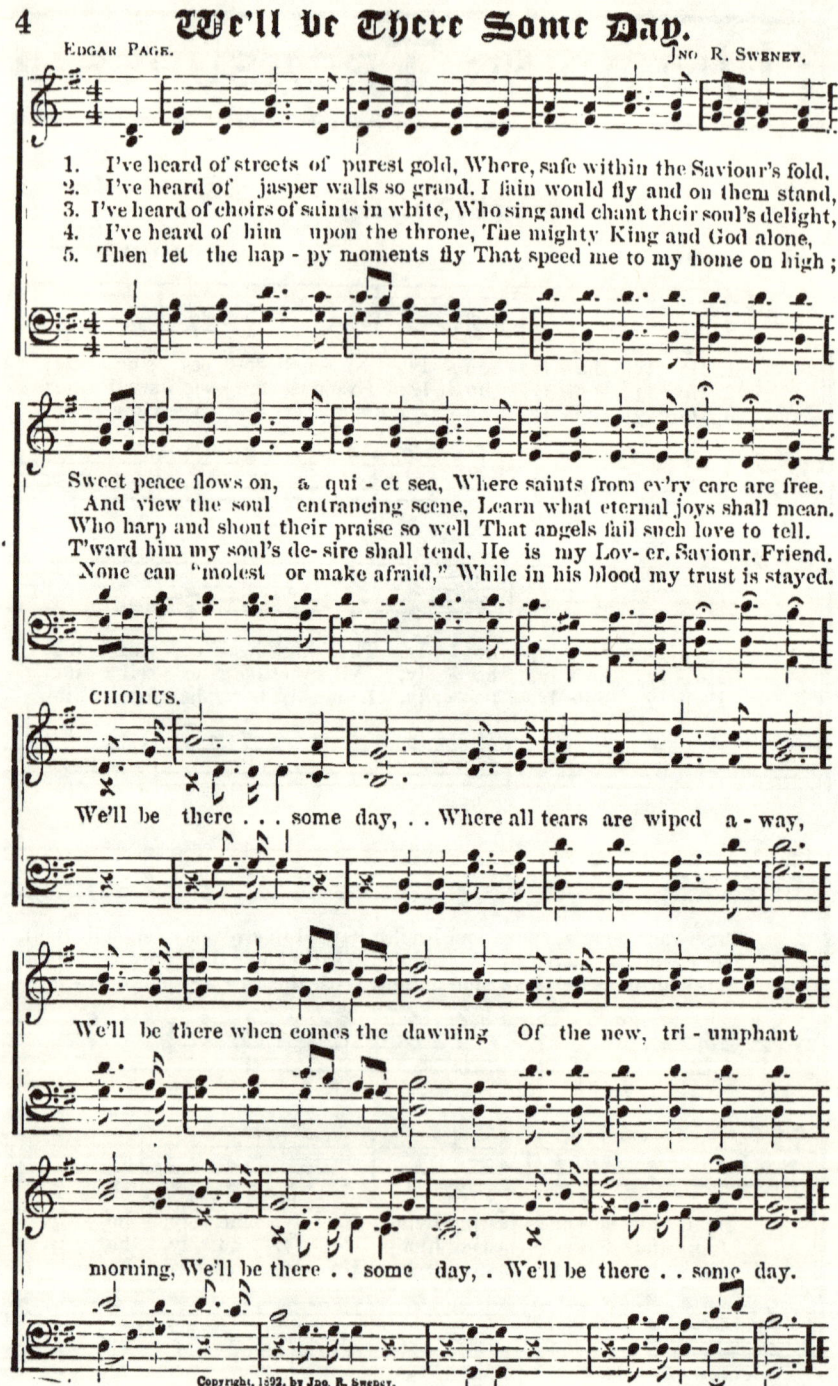

All for Jesus.

MARY D. JAMES. JNO. R. SWENEY.

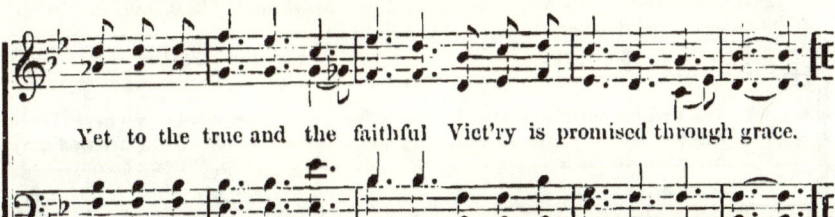

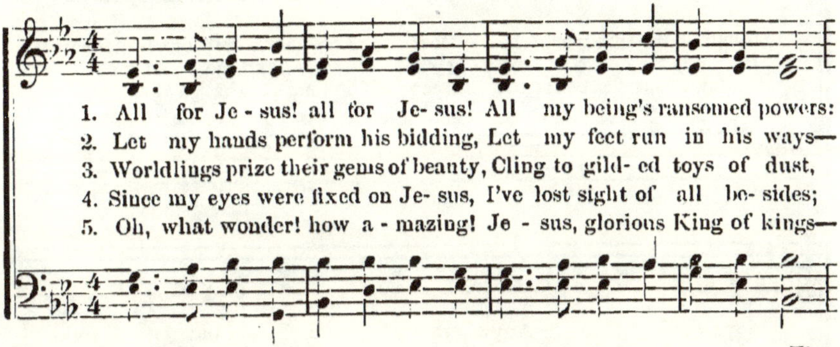

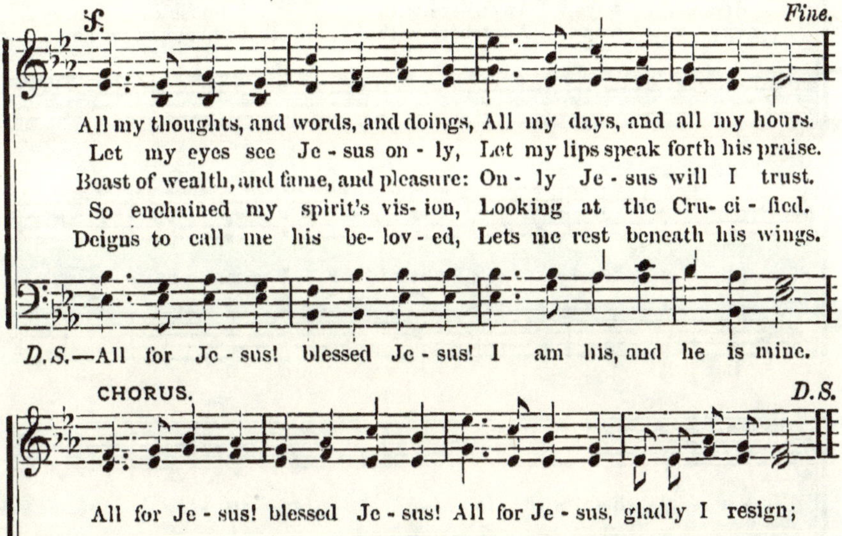

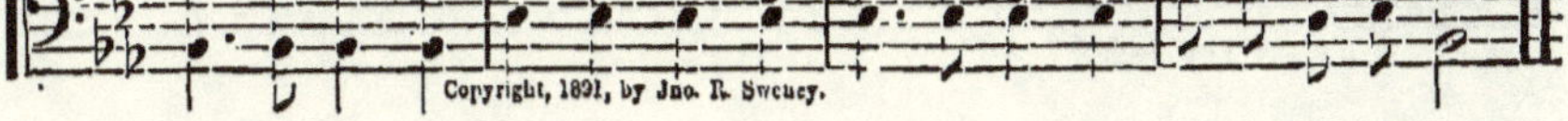

Glory, He Saves!

F A. B. F. A. BLACKMER.

1. Glo-ry to Jesus, he saves e-ven me! All my guilt nail-ing to Cal-va-ry's tree; Paid is the debt and my soul is set free, Glo-ry to Je-sus, he saves!
2. Wand'ring he found me a-far from the fold, Per-ish-ing there in the dark-ness and cold; Half of his good-ness can nev-er be told, Glo-ry to Je-sus, he saves!
3. Safe-ly and sweet-ly he keeps me each day, Gent-ly, so gent-ly he leads all the way; An-swers of peace sends he down when I pray, Glo-ry to Je-sus, he saves!
4. Bless-ed com-pan-ion-ship! cheer-ing 'me so! Sweet-er and sweet-er each day shall it grow, Till to be like him I joy-ful-ly go, Glo-ry to Je-sus, he saves!

CHORUS.

Glo-ry, he saves! wondrously saves! Saves a poor sinner like me; Glo-ry, he saves! wondrously saves! Glo-ry to Je-sus, he saves!

Copyright, 1890, in "Singing by the Way."

10 Plenty to Do.

Words from "Wesleyan Juvenile Offering." T. C. O'KANE. By per.
In moderate time.

1. "Go, work in my vineyard, there's plenty to do, The harvest is great and the lab'rers are few;" I've sheep to be tended and lambs to be fed, The lost must be gathered, the weary ones led.
2. "Go, work in my vineyard," I claim thee as mine, With blood did I buy thee, and all that is thine, Thy time and thy talents, thy loftiest powers, Thy warmest affections, thy sunniest hours.
3. "Go, work in my vineyard," oh, "work while 'tis day," The bright hours of sunshine are hast'ning away, And night's gloomy shadows are gathering fast; The time for our la-bor shall ev-er be past.
4. "Go, work in my vineyard," and toil all the day, Thy strength I'll sup-ply, and thy wages I'll pay, And blessed, thrice blessed the dil-igent few, Who'll finish the la-bor I've giv'n them to do.

CHORUS.

Go, work, ... go, work, ... Go, work in my vineyard, there's plenty to do; Go, work, ... go work, The harvest is great and the lab'rers are few.

Go, work in my vineyard, go, work in my vineyard, Go, work, work, work, work,

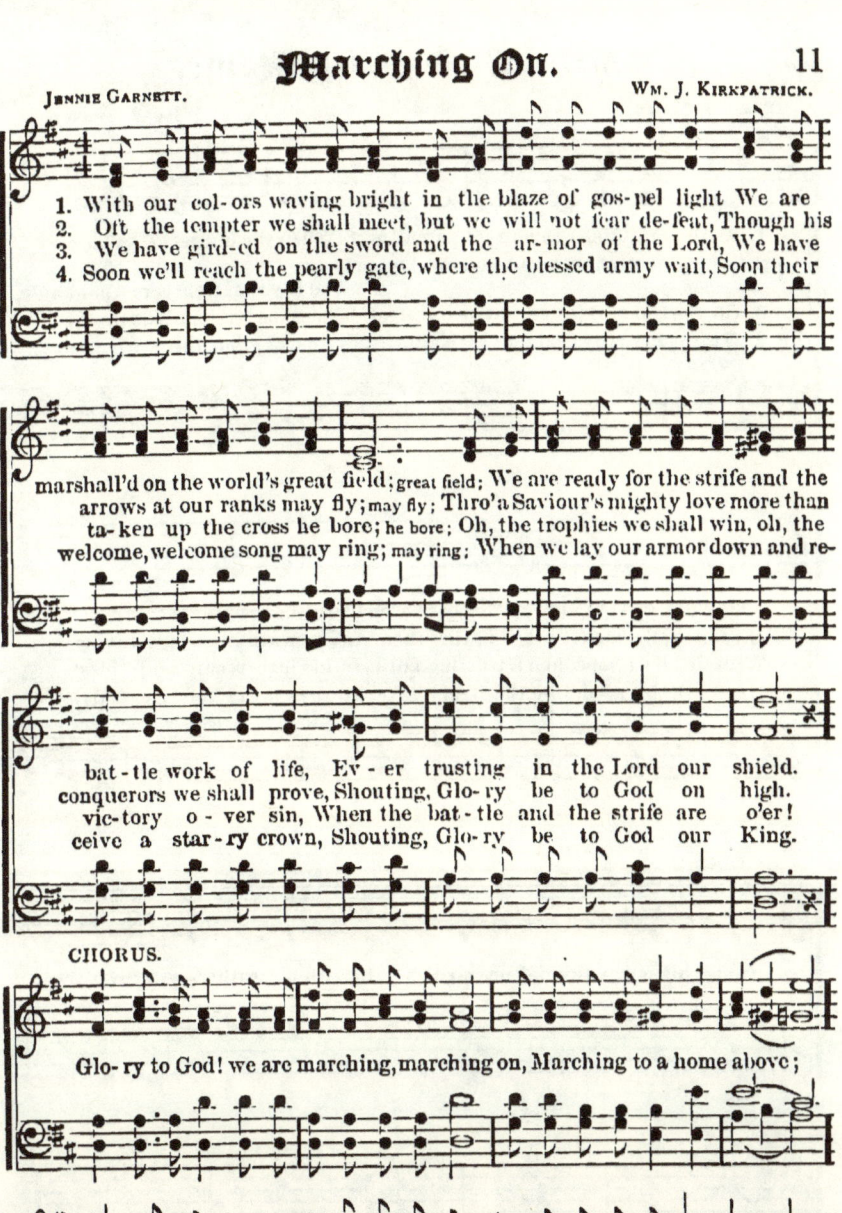

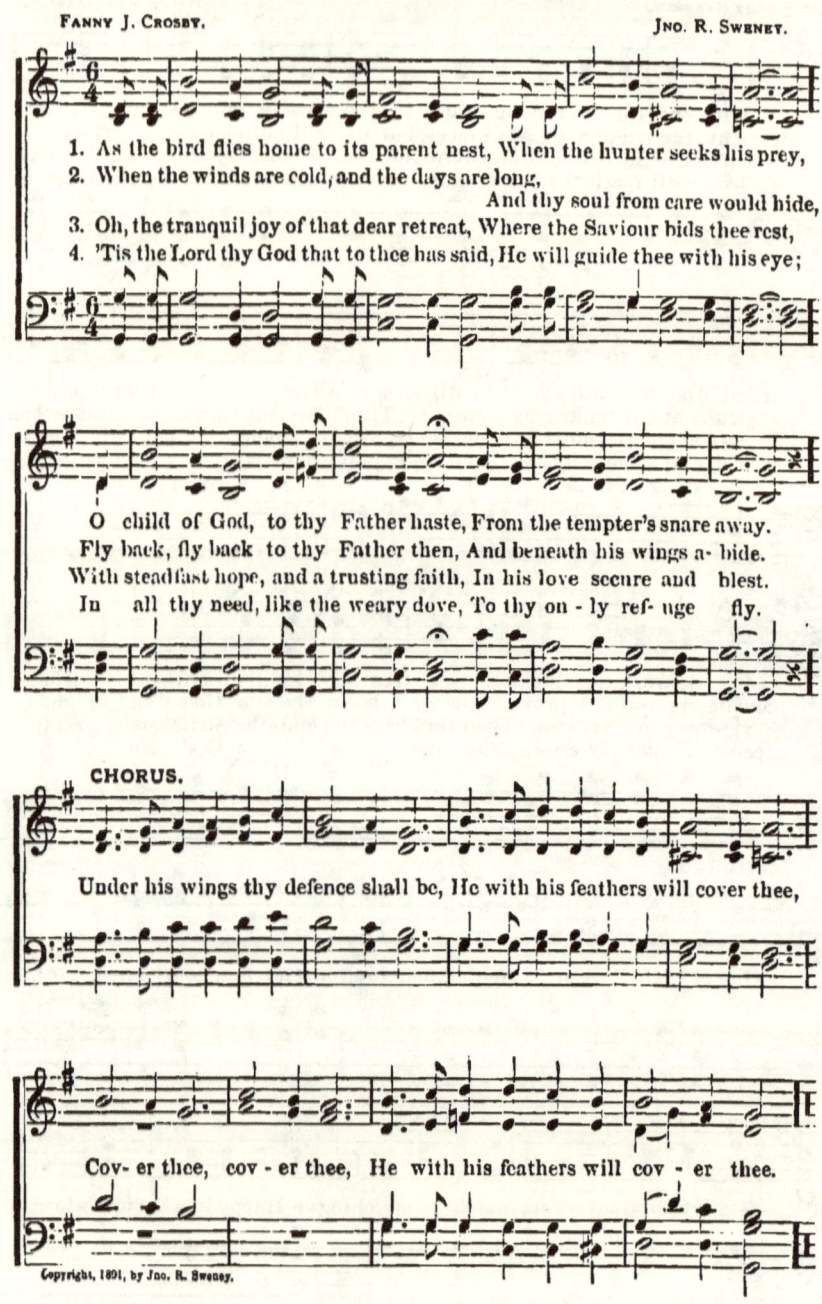

4 But we never can prove
  The delights of his love
Until all on the altar we lay,
  For the favor he shows,
  And the joy he bestows,
Are for all who will trust and obey.

5 Then in fellowship sweet
  We will sit at his feet,
Or we'll walk by his side in the way;
  What he says we will do,
  Where he sends we will go,
Never fear, only trust and obey.

18. We'll Never Say Good By.

"We shall never say 'good by' in heaven."—The words of a dying Christian woman.

Mrs. E. W. Chapman.   J. H. Tenney.

1. Our friends on earth we meet with pleasure, While swift the moments fly,
2. How joyful is the thought that lingers, When loved ones cross death's sea,
3. No parting words shall e'er be spoken In that bright land of flowers,

Yet ev - er comes the thought of sadness That we must say good by.
That when our la - bors here are end - ed, With them we'll ev - er be.
But songs of joy, and peace, and gladness, Shall ev - ermore be ours.

CHORUS.

We'll nev-er say good by in heaven, We'll never say good by, . . .

Repeat Chorus pp

For in that land of joy and song We'll never say good by.

Copyright, 1868, by John J. Hood.

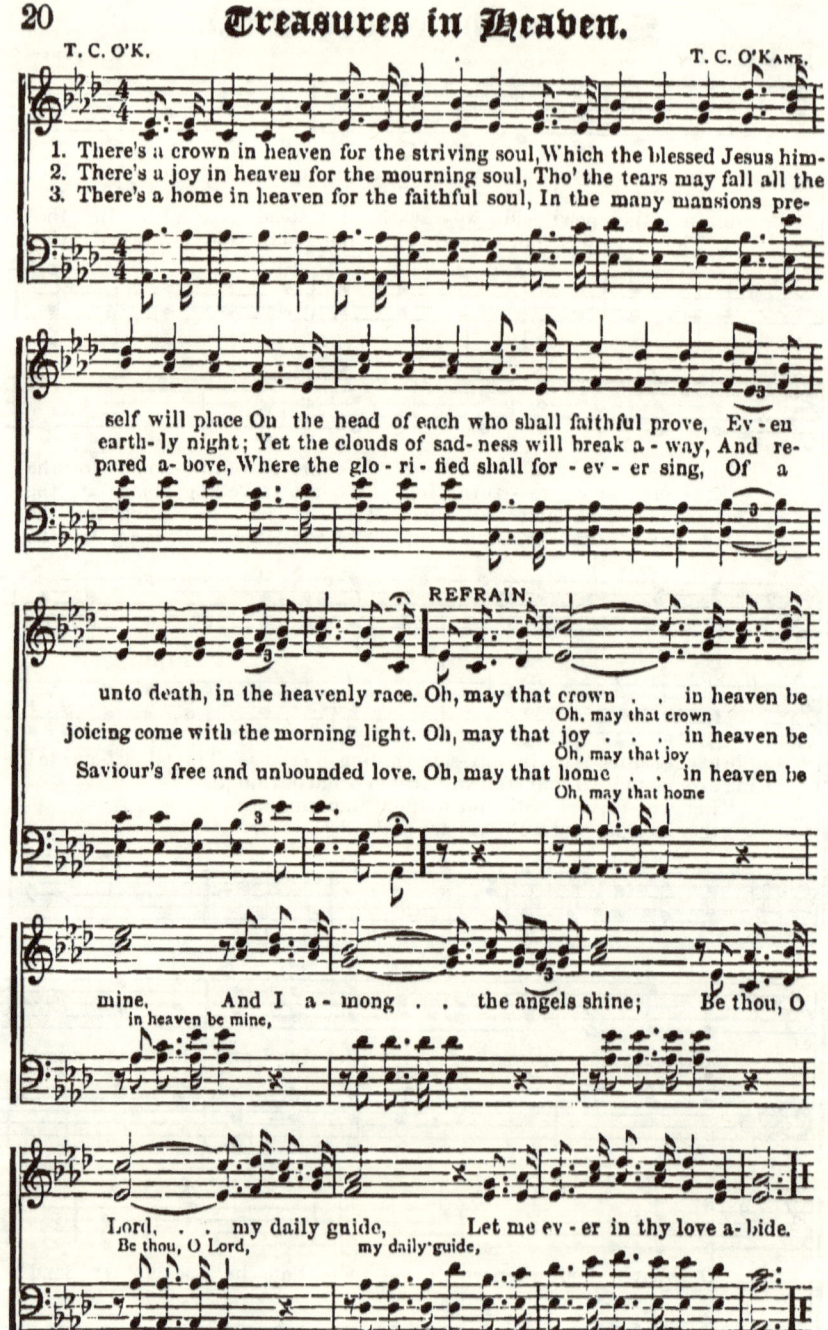

The Sure Foundation.

T. C. O'Kane.

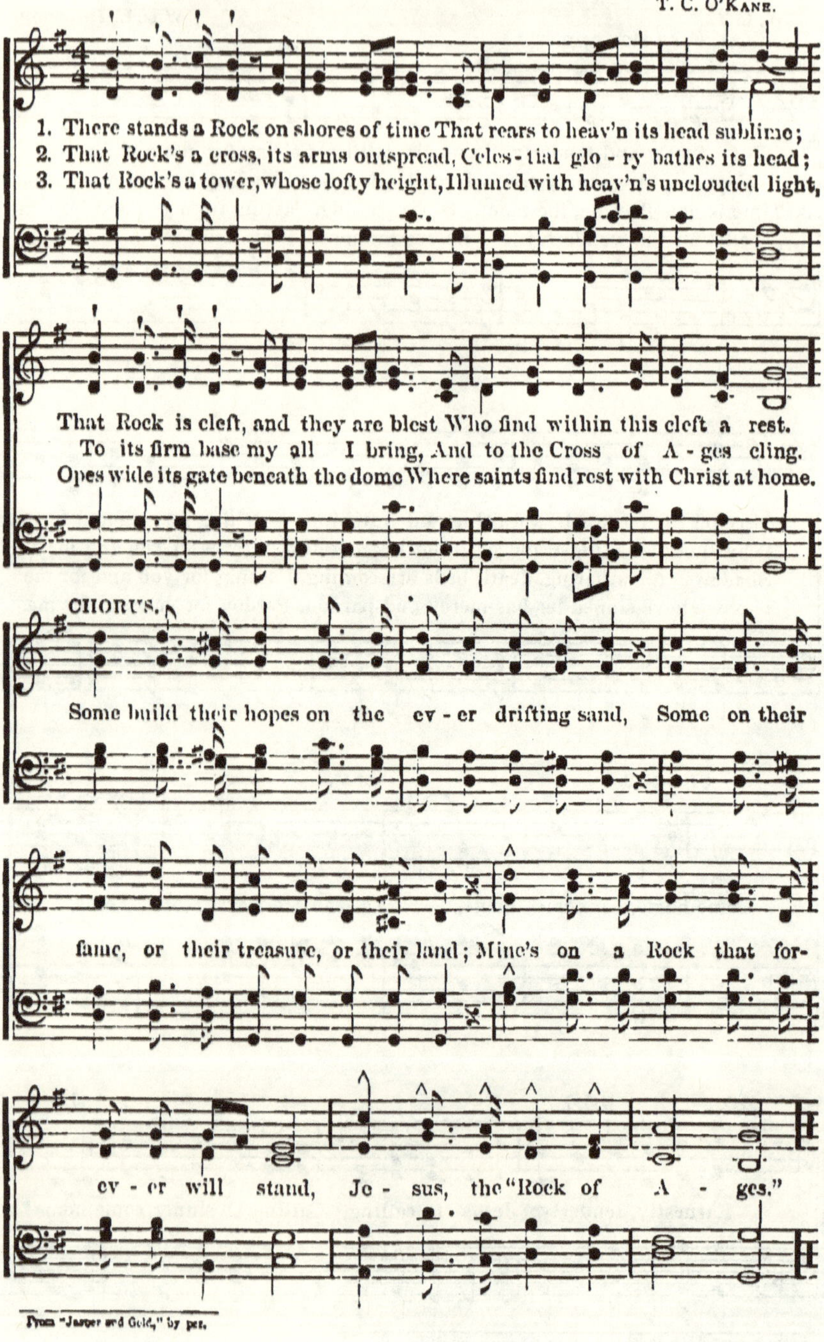

From "Jasper and Gold," by per.

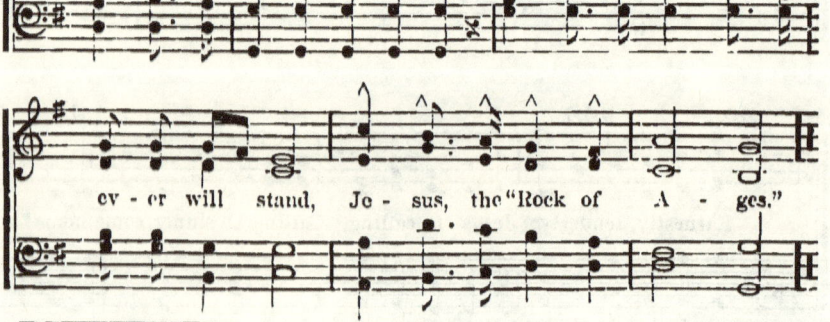

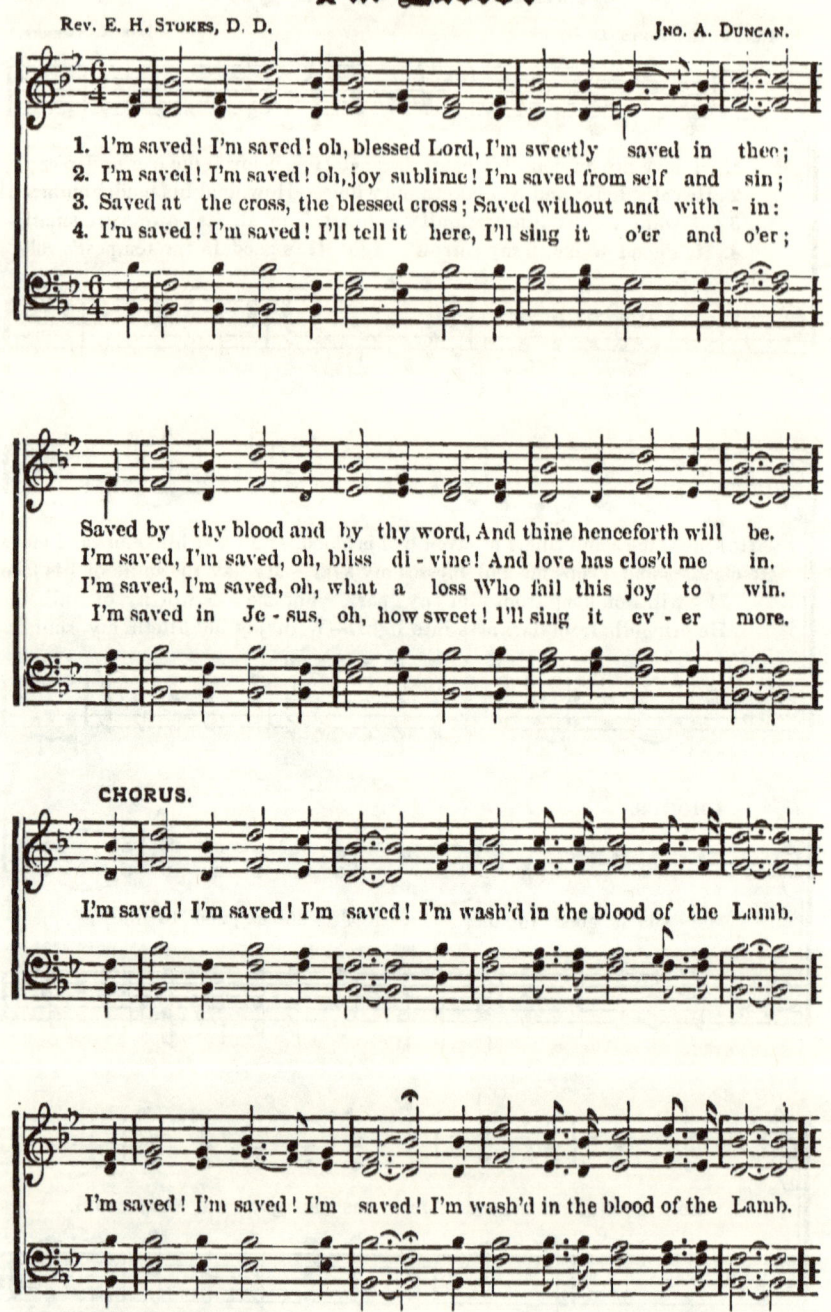

He'll Mention Them, etc.—CONCLUDED.

sins are all tak-en a-way, tak-en a-way. tak-en a-way.

Lord, I'm Coming Home.

W. J. K.   *With great feeling.*   Wm. J. Kirkpatrick.

1. I've wandered far a-way from God, Now I'm coming home;
2. I've wast-ed ma-ny pre-cious years, Now I'm coming home;
3. I'm tired of sin and stray-ing, Lord, Now I'm coming home;
4. My soul is sick, my heart is sore, Now I'm coming home;

The paths of sin too long I've trod, Lord, I'm coming home.
I now re-pent with bit-ter tears, Lord, I'm coming home.
I'll trust thy love, be-lieve thy word, Lord, I'm coming home.
My strength renew, my hope re-store, Lord, I'm coming home.

D.S.—O-pen wide thine arms of love, Lord, I'm coming home.

CHORUS.

Coming home, coming home, Nev-er more to roam;

Copyright, 1892, by Wm. J. Kirkpatrick.

5 My only hope, my only plea,
   Now I'm coming home,
That Jesus died, and died for me,
   Lord, I'm coming home.

6 I need his cleansing blood I know,
   Now I'm coming home;
Oh, wash me whiter than the snow,
   Lord, I'm coming home.

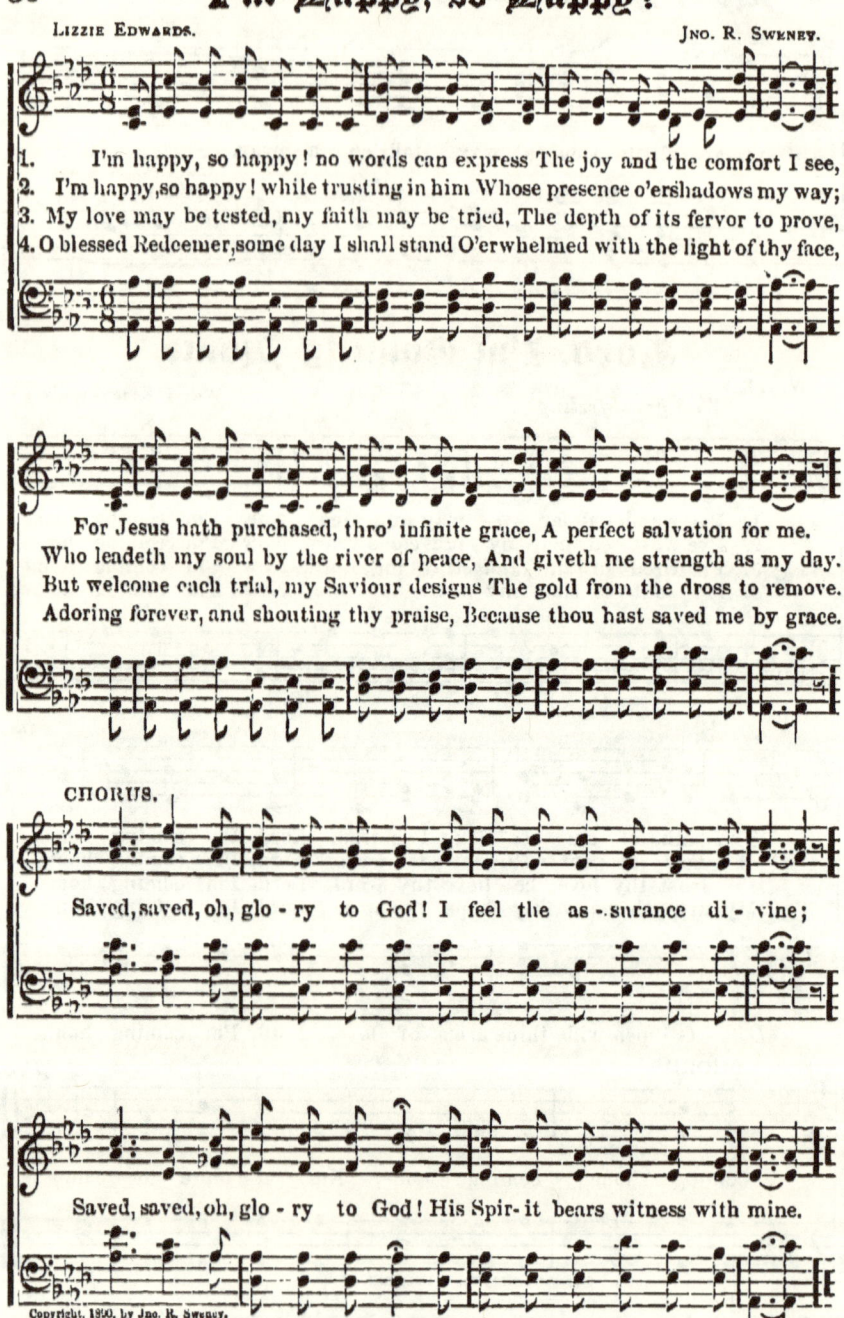

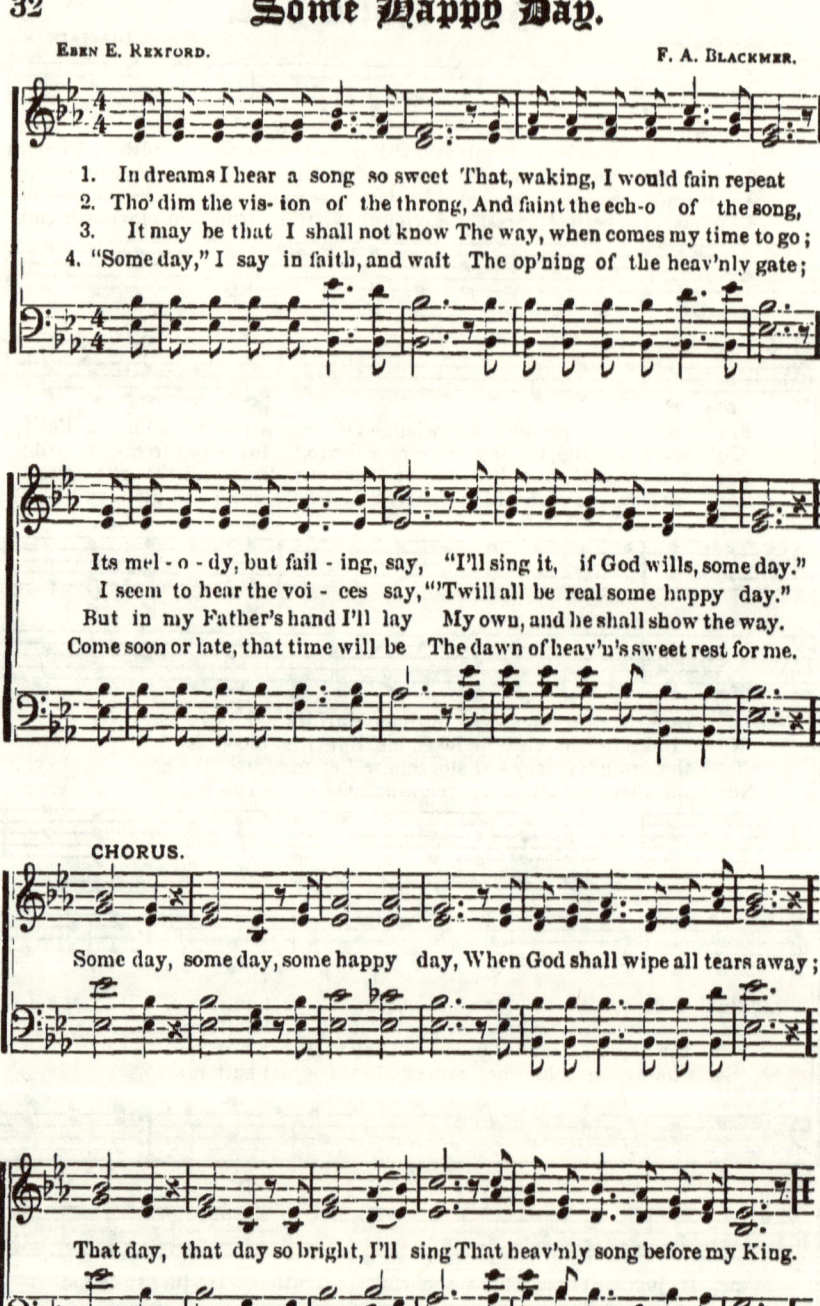

34. Help Just a Little.

Music from "The Wells of Salvation," new words by Rev. W. A. Spencer.

Wm. J. Kirkpatrick.

1. Brother for Christ's kingdom sighing, Help a lit-tle, help a lit-tle;
2. Is thy cup made sad by tri-al? Help a lit-tle, help a lit-tle;
3. Though no wealth to thee is giv-en, Help a lit-tle, help a lit-tle;

Help to save the mil-lions dy-ing, Help just a lit-tle.
Sweet-en it with self-de-ni-al, Help just a lit-tle.
Sac-ri-fice is gold in heav-en, Help just a lit-tle.

CHORUS.

Oh, the wrongs that we may righten! Oh, the hearts that we may lighten!

Oh, the skies that we may brighten! Helping just a lit-tle.

4 Let us live for one another,
Help a little, help a little;
Help to lift each fallen brother,
Help just a little.

5 Tho' thy life is pressed with sorrow,
Help a little, help a little;
Bravely look t'ward God's to-morrow.
Help just a little.

Copyright, 1885, by John J. Hood.

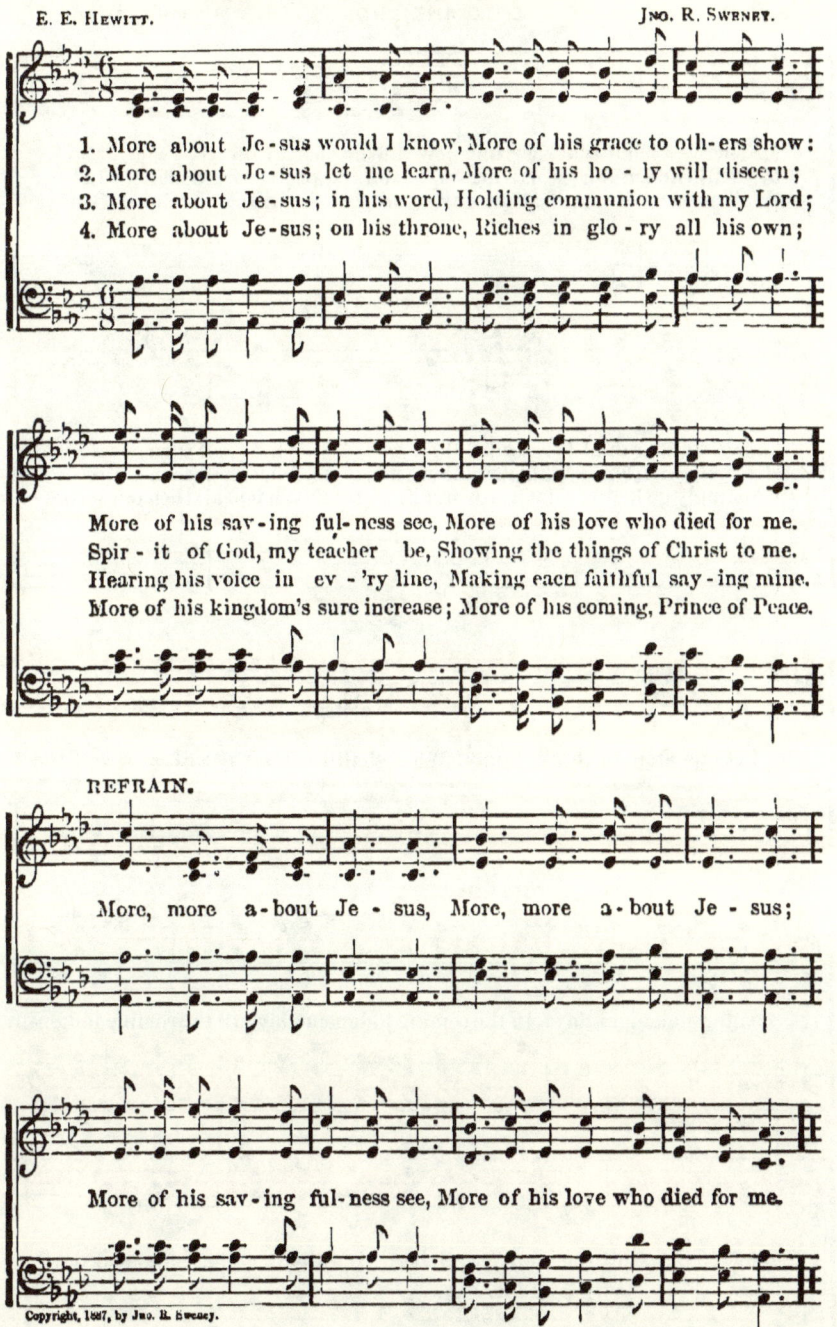

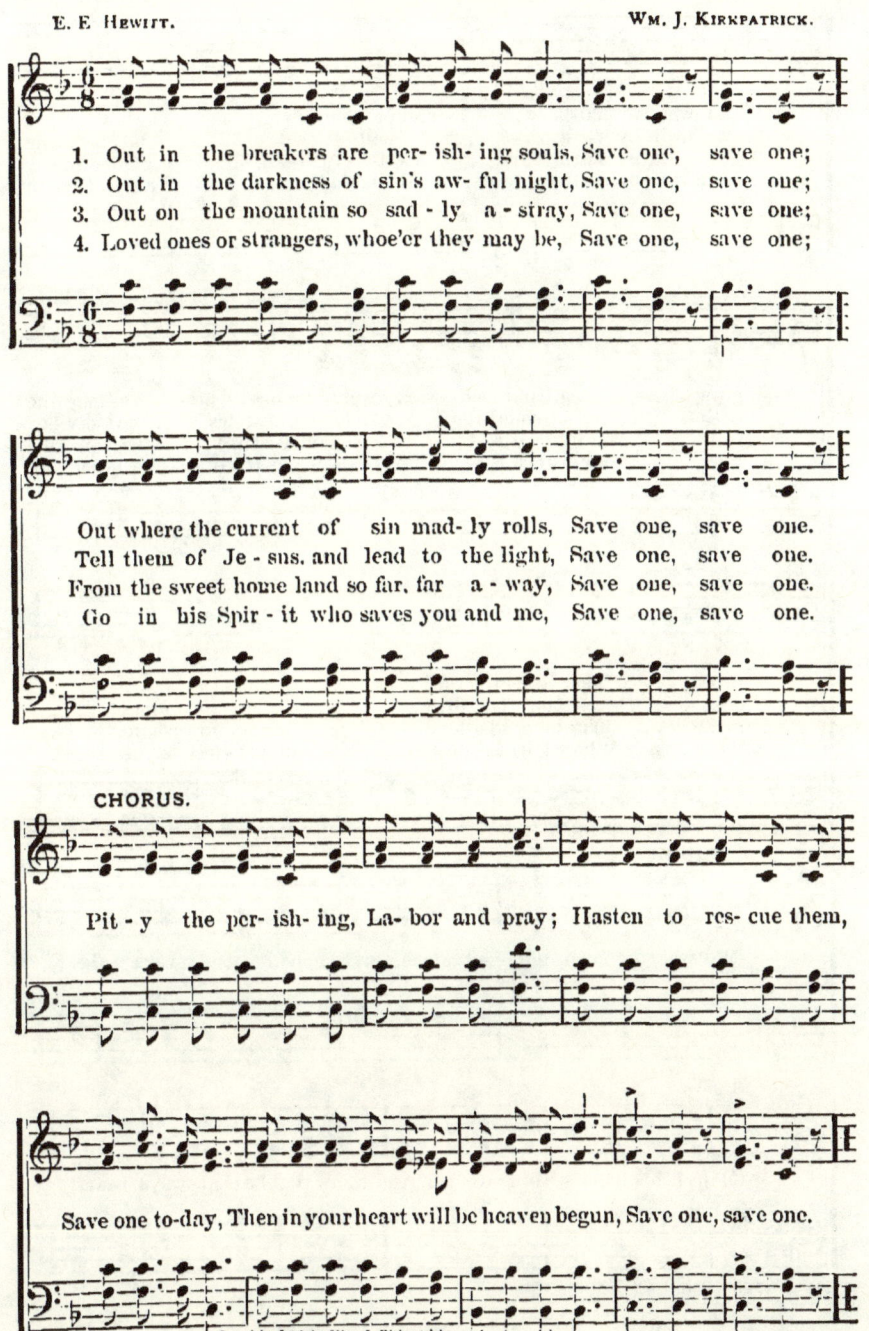

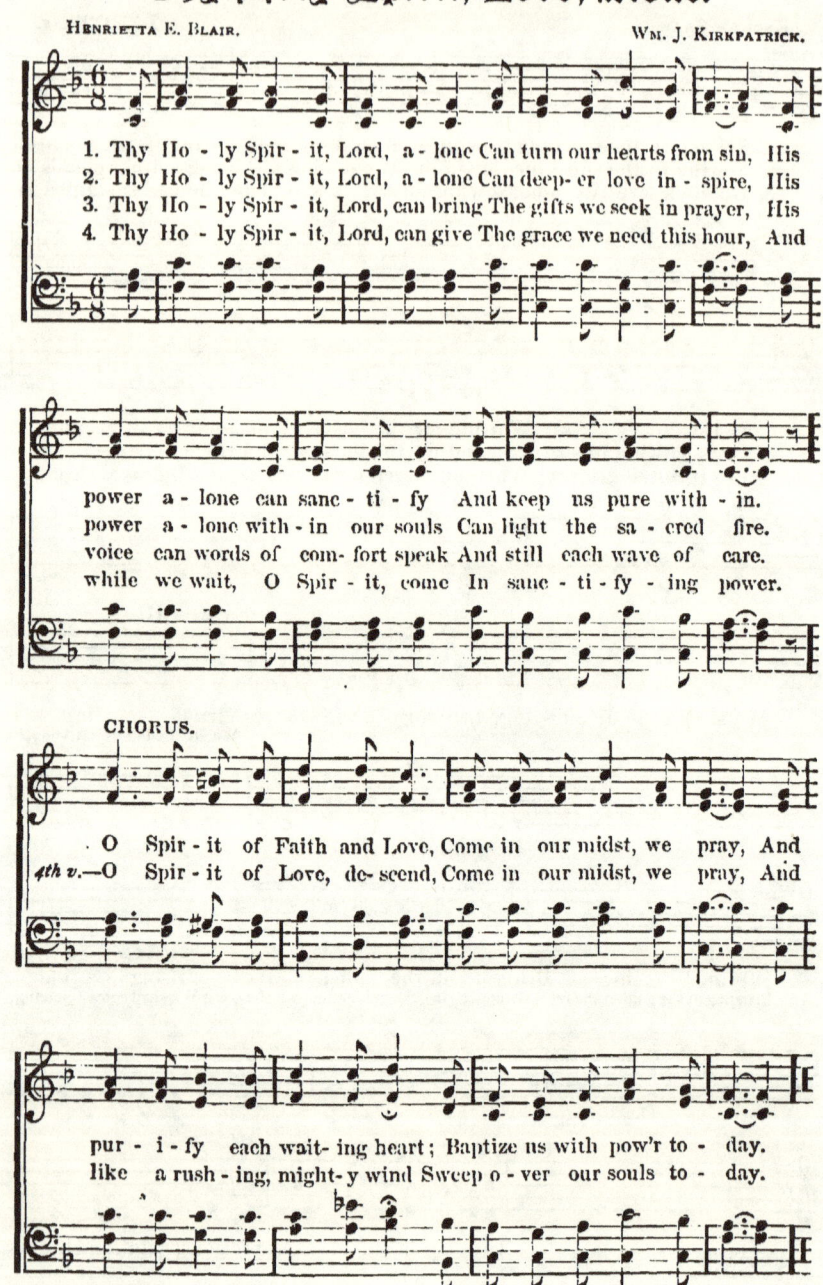

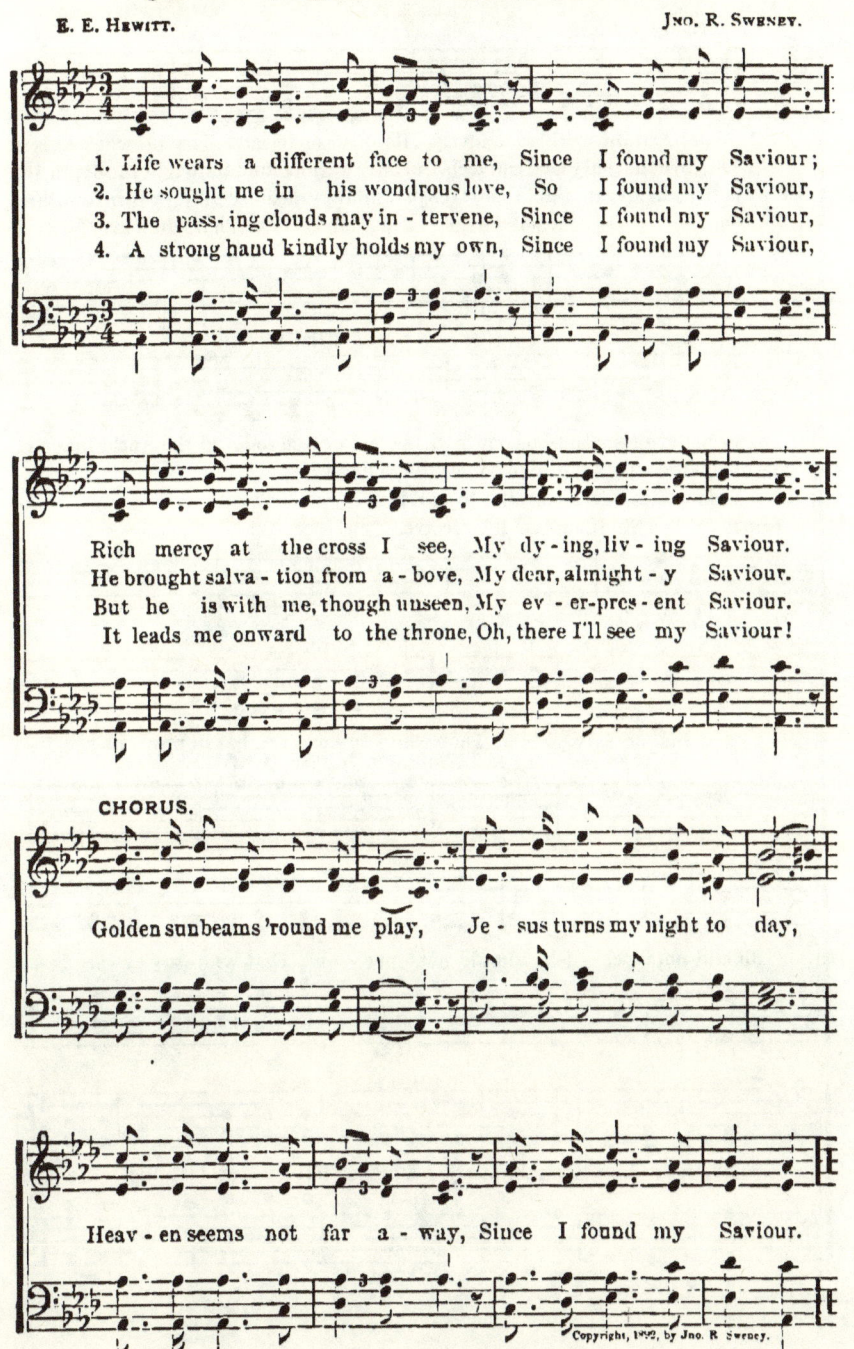

42. God so Loved the World.

Fanny J. Crosby.   John iii. 16.   Wm. J. Kirkpatrick.

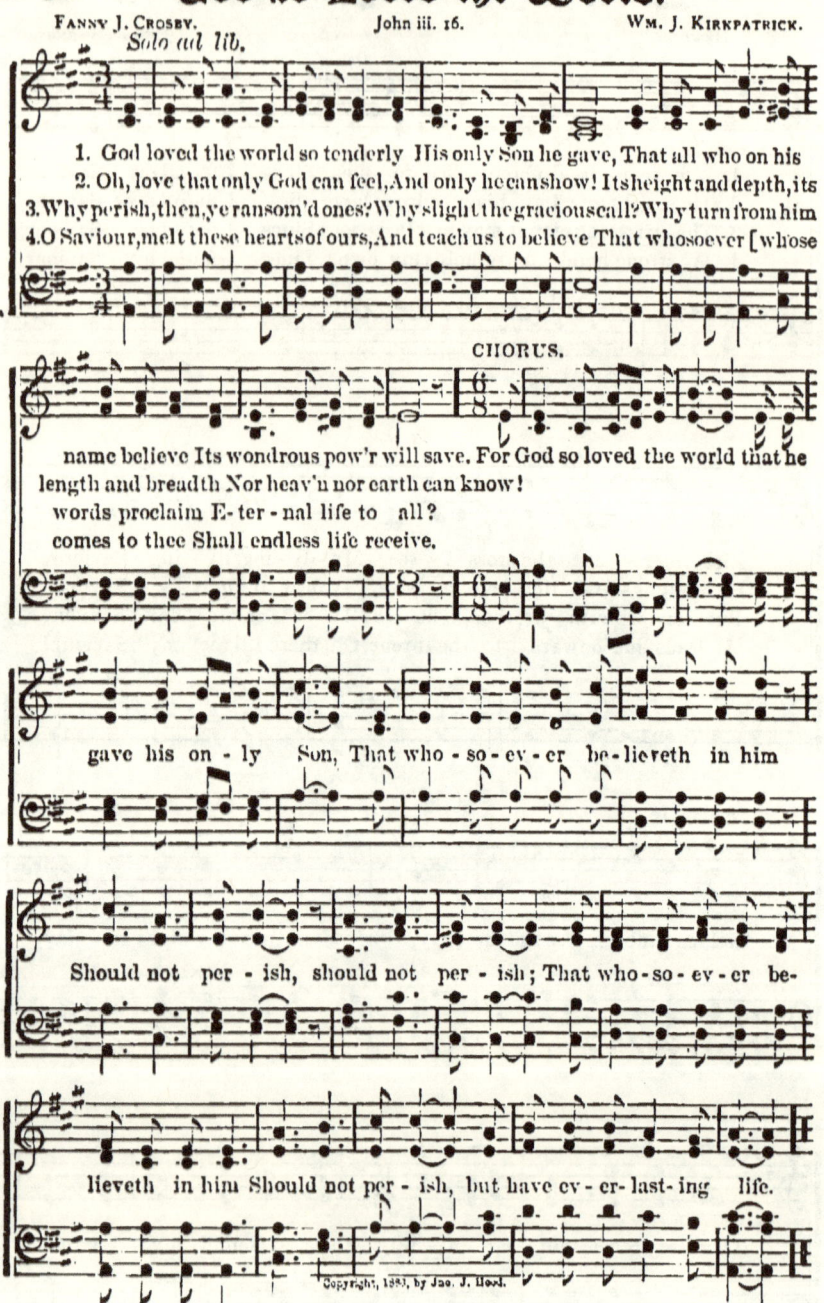

Solo ad lib.

1. God loved the world so tenderly His only Son he gave, That all who on his
2. Oh, love that only God can feel, And only he can show! Its height and depth, its
3. Why perish, then, ye ransom'd ones? Why slight the gracious call? Why turn from him
4. O Saviour, melt these hearts of ours, And teach us to believe That whosoever [whose

name believe Its wondrous pow'r will save. For God so loved the world that he
length and breadth Nor heav'n nor earth can know!
words proclaim E-ter-nal life to all?
comes to thee Shall endless life receive.

CHORUS.

gave his on-ly Son, That who-so-ev-er be-lieveth in him Should not per-ish, should not per-ish; That who-so-ev-er be-lieveth in him Should not per-ish, but have ev-er-last-ing life.

Copyright, 1883, by Jno. J. Hood.

O Christian, Awake! 45

"Stand, therefore, having your loins girt about with truth, and having on the breastplate of righteousness."

Arr. from "Singing Pilgrim."

1. O Christian, a-wake! for the strife is at hand, With helmet and shield
2. Whatev- er thy danger, take heed and beware, And turn not thy back,
3. The cause of thy Master with vig- or defend; O watch, fight, and pray—
4. Press on, nev- er doubting; thy Captain is near, With grace to supply,

and a sword in thy hand; To meet the bold tempter, go, fearless- ly go,
for no ar- mor is there; The legions of darkness if thou would'st o'erthrow,
persevere to the end; Wherev- er he leads thee, go, valiant- ly go,
and with comfort to cheer; His love, like a stream, in the desert will flow,

REFRAIN.

And stand like the brave, with thy face to the foe. Stand like the brave,
Then stand like the brave, with thy face to the foe.
And stand like the brave, with thy face to the foe.
Then stand like the brave, with thy face to the foe. Stand like the brave,

Stand like the brave, Stand like the brave, with thy face to the foe.
Stand like the brave,

By permission.

Only Remembered.

H. Bonar, D.D.
Jno. R. Sweney.

1. Fading away, like the dew of the morning, Soaring from earth to its
2. Shall I be missed if an-oth-er succeed me, Reaping the fields I in
3. Oh, when the Saviour shall make up his jewels, When the bright crowns of re-

home in the sun: Thus would I pass from the earth and its toil-ing,
spring-time have sown? No, for the sow-er may pass from his la-bors,
joic-ing are won, Then will his faith-ful and wea-ry dis-ci-ples,

CHORUS.

On - ly remembered by what I have done. On - ly remembered,
On - ly remembered by what he has done.
All be remembered for what they have done.

only remembered, Only remembered by what I have done, Only remembered,

rit.

on - ly remembered, On - ly remem-bered by what I have done.

Copyright, 1886, by John J. Hood.

Entire Consecration.

FRANCES RIDLEY HAVERGAL.   Chorus by W. J. K.   WM. J. KIRKPATRICK.

1. Take my life, and let it be Con-se-crat-ed, Lord, to thee;
2. Take my feet, and let them be Swift and beau-ti-ful for thee;
3. Take my lips, and let them be Filled with mes-sag-es for thee;
4. Take my moments and my days, Let them flow in endless praise;

Take my hands and let them move At the impulse of thy love.
Take my voice and let me sing Al-ways, on-ly, for my King.
Take my sil-ver and my gold,— Not a mite would I withhold.
Take my in-tel-lect, and use Ev-'ry power as thou shalt choose.

CHORUS.

Wash me in the Saviour's precious blood, the precious blood,
Cleanse me in its pu-ri-fy-ing flood, the healing flood,
Lord, I give to thee, my life and all, to be, Thine, henceforth, e-ter-nal-ly.

5 Take my will, and make it thine;
It shall be no longer mine;
Take my heart.—it is thine own,—
It shall be thy royal throne.

6 Take my love,—my Lord, I pour
At thy feet its treasure-store!
Take myself, and I will be
Ever, only, all for thee!

Copyright, by Wm. J. Kirkpatrick.

The Stranger at the Door.

Rev. iii. 20. — T. C. O'Kane.

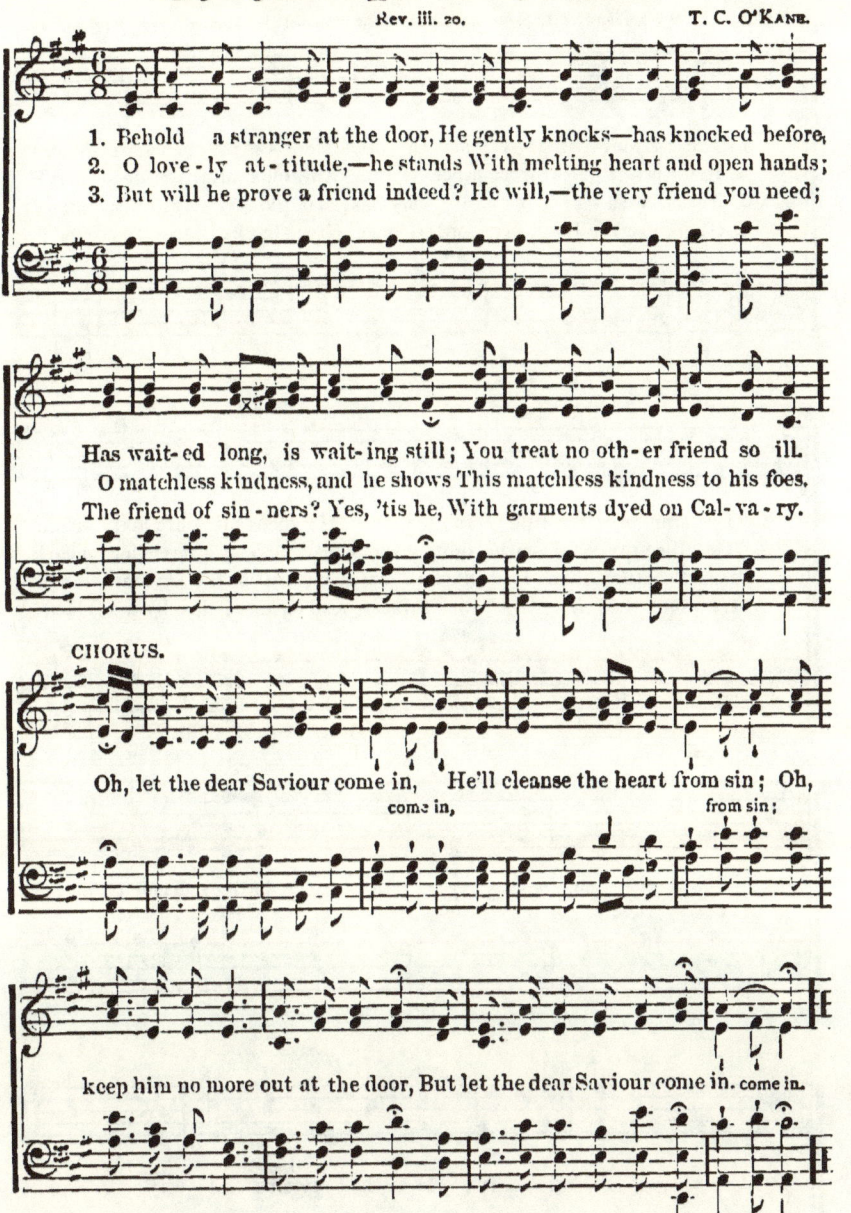

1. Behold a stranger at the door, He gently knocks—has knocked before, Has waited long, is waiting still; You treat no other friend so ill.
2. O lovely attitude,—he stands With melting heart and open hands; O matchless kindness, and he shows This matchless kindness to his foes.
3. But will he prove a friend indeed? He will,—the very friend you need; The friend of sinners? Yes, 'tis he, With garments dyed on Calvary.

CHORUS.
Oh, let the dear Saviour come in, He'll cleanse the heart from sin; Oh, keep him no more out at the door, But let the dear Saviour come in.

4 Rise, touched with gratitude divine,
Turn out his enemy and thine;
That soul-destroying monster, Sin,
And let the heavenly Stranger in.

5 Admit him, ere his anger burn,—
His feet, departed, ne'er return;
Admit him, or the hour's at hand
You'll at HIS door rejected stand.

4   *Unfading Treasures*—D

50. The Saviour is My All in All.

P. B.   "Wherefore he is able to save them to the uttermost."—Heb. vii. 25.   P. Bilhorn.

1. The Saviour is my all in all, He is my constant theme!
2. His Spir-it gives sweet peace within, And bids all care de-part!
3. And whatso-ev-er I may ask, To glo-ri-fy his name,
4. Oh, praise the Lord, my soul, rejoice, Give thanks unto thy God!

By sim-ply trusting in his word He keeps me pure and clean.
He fills my soul with righteousness, And pu-ri-fies the heart.
The Fa-ther free-ly gives to me, Since Christ the Saviour came.
Who took thee in thy sin-fulness, And cleansed thee by his blood!

CHORUS.
Glo-ry! oh, glo-ry! Je-sus hath redeemed me;
Glo-ry! oh, glo-ry! He washed my sins a-way, a-way!

Copyright, 1886, by P. Bilhorn.

Harvest Time.—CONCLUDED.

A Sinner like Me.

C. J. B.   Chas. J. Butler.

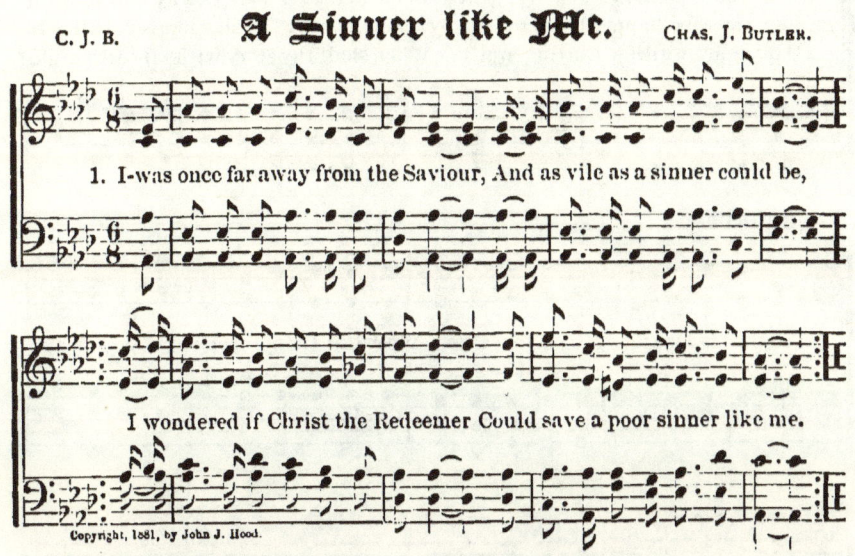

Copyright, 1881, by John J. Hood.

2 I wandered on in the darkness,
  Not a ray of light could I see, [ness,
And the thought filled my heart with sad-
  There's no hope for a sinner like me.

3 I then fully trusted in Jesus,
  And oh, what a joy came to me;
My heart was filled with his praises,
  For saving a sinner like me.

4 No longer in darkness I'm walking,
  For the light is now shining on me,
And now unto others I'm telling,
  How he saved a poor sinner like me.

5 And when life's journey is over,
  And I the dear Saviour shall see,
I'll praise him for ever and ever,
  For saving a sinner like me.

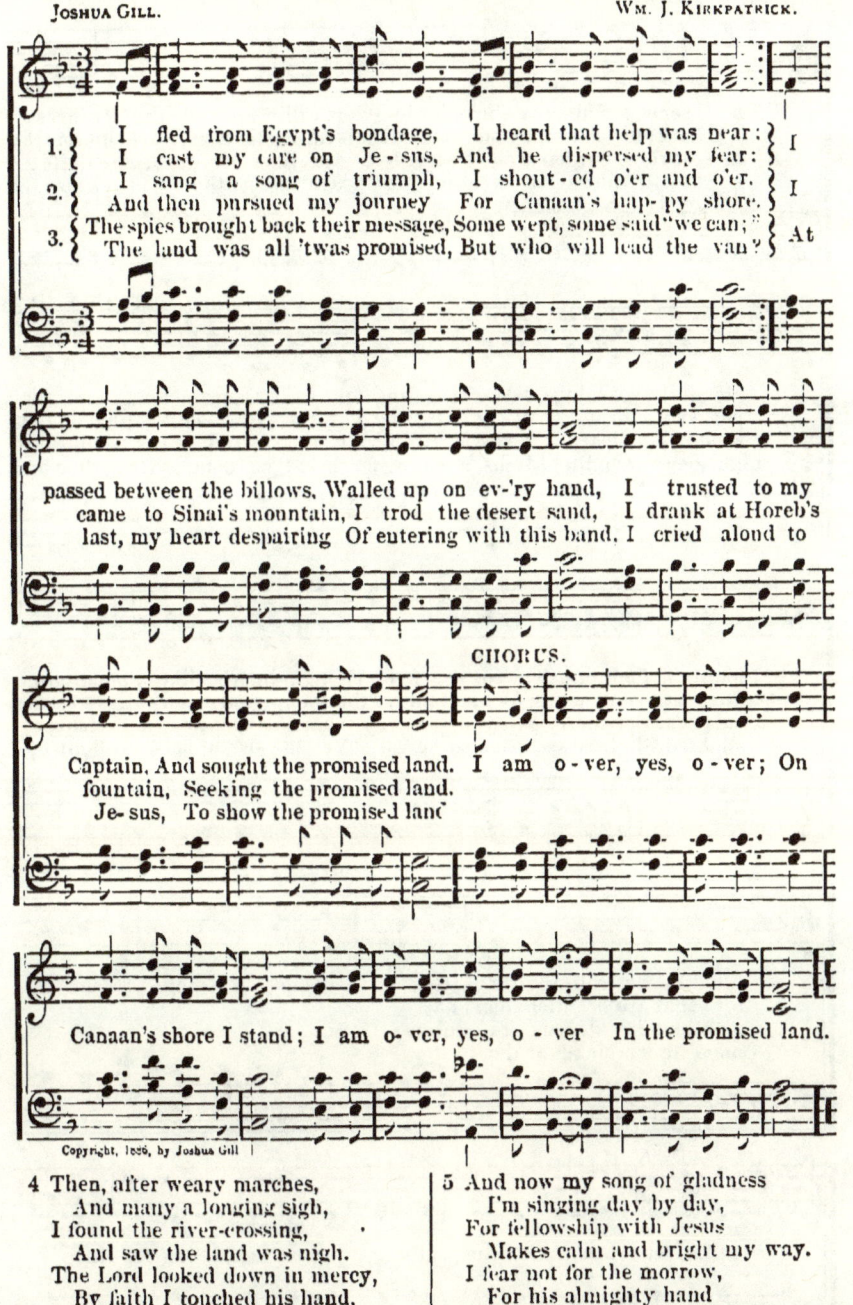

4 Then, after weary marches,
   And many a longing sigh,
  I found the river-crossing,
   And saw the land was nigh.
  The Lord looked down in mercy,
   By faith I touched his hand,
  I followed close beside him,
   And found the promised land.

5 And now my song of gladness
   I'm singing day by day,
  For fellowship with Jesus
   Makes calm and bright my way.
  I fear not for the morrow,
   For his almighty hand
  I know shall lead and keep me
   In this the promised land.

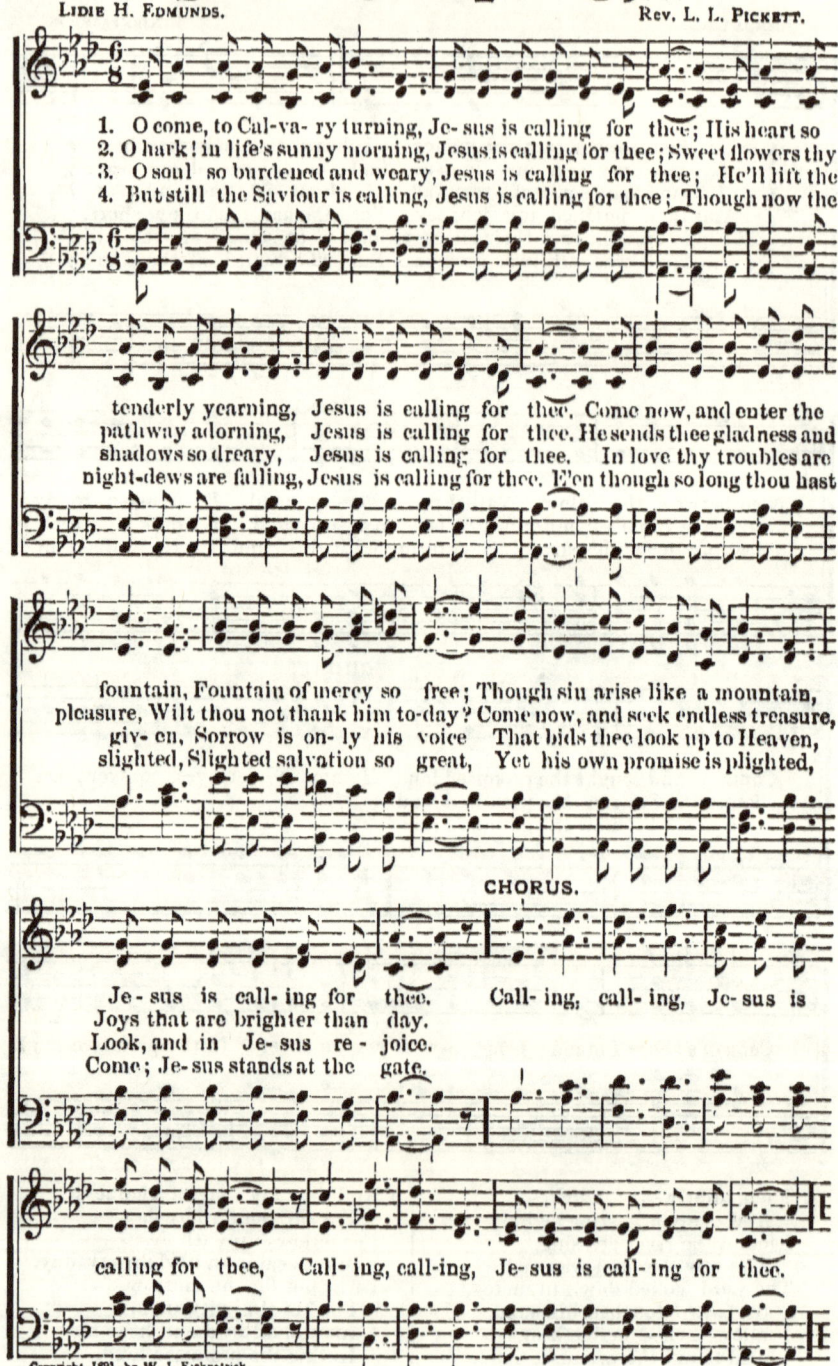

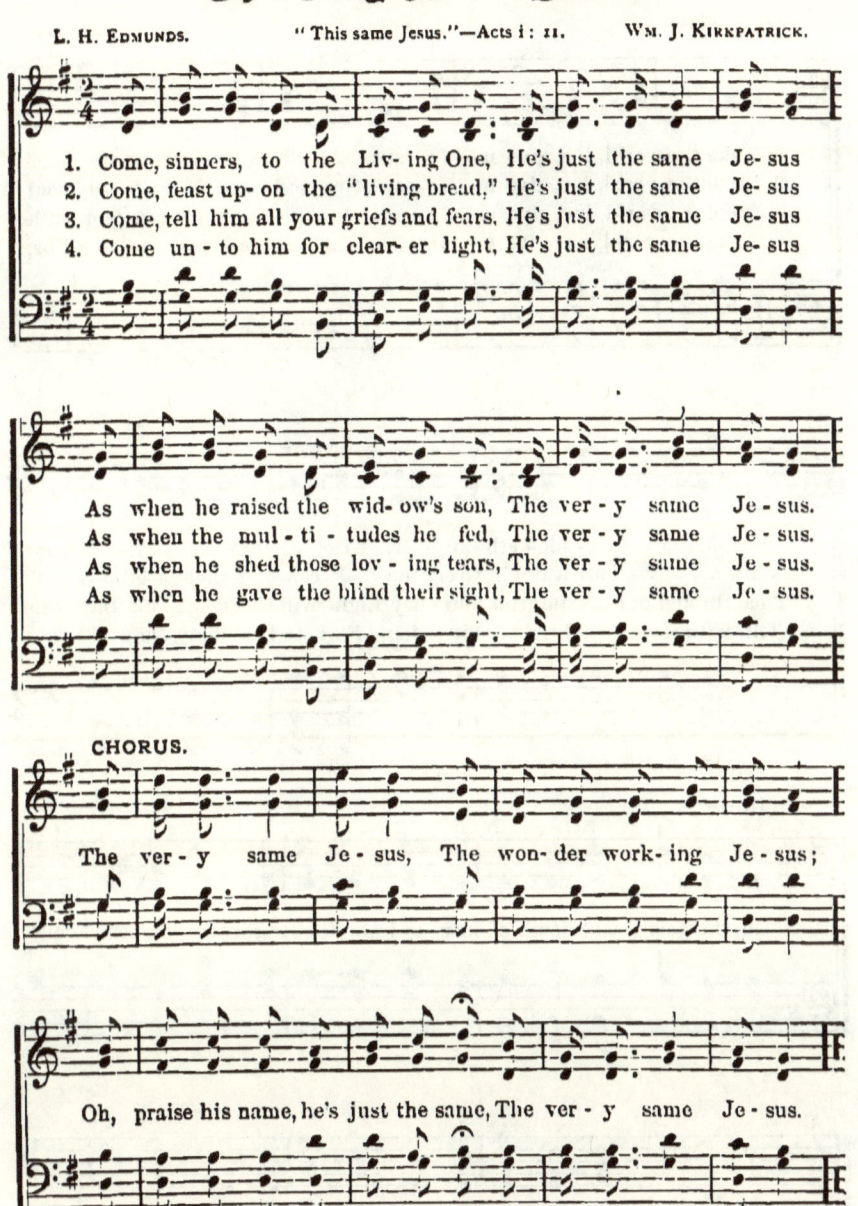

5 Calm 'midst the waves of trouble be,
   He's just the same Jesus
   As when he hushed the raging sea,
   The very same Jesus.

6 Some day our raptured eyes shall see
   He's just the same Jesus;
   Oh, blessed day for you and me!
   The very same Jesus.

The Lights of Home.—CONCLUDED. 63

There, ... beyond the billows foam, We see the lights of home.
There, beyond, beyond

Brought Back.

H. L. Gilmour.   Arr. by J. J. H.

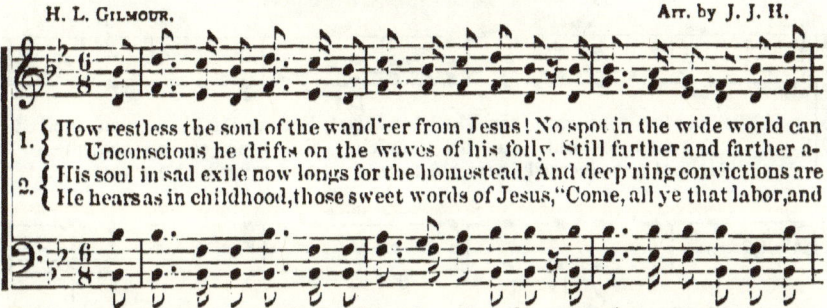

1. { How restless the soul of the wand'rer from Jesus! No spot in the wide world can
    Unconscious he drifts on the waves of his folly. Still farther and farther a-
2. { His soul in sad exile now longs for the homestead, And deep'ning convictions are
    He hears as in childhood, those sweet words of Jesus,"Come, all ye that labor, and

D. C.—And chords of "sweet home," that have long been reposing,
                                             By fingers unseen are a-
D. C. He ventures in weakness, but strength is imparted, And gladly he's welcomed by

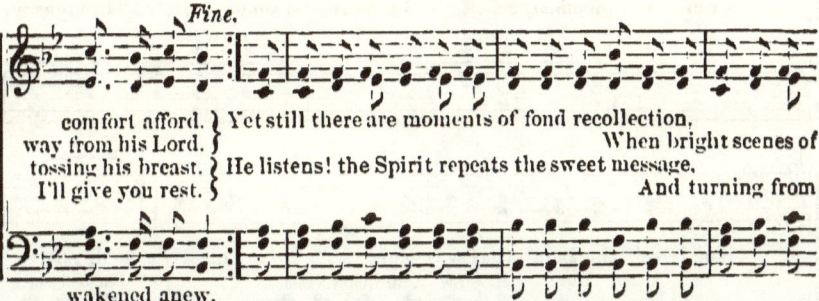

comfort afford. } Yet still there are moments of fond recollection,
way from his Lord. }   When bright scenes of
tossing his breast. } He listens! the Spirit repeats the sweet message,
I'll give you rest. }   And turning from

wakened anew.
Father at home.

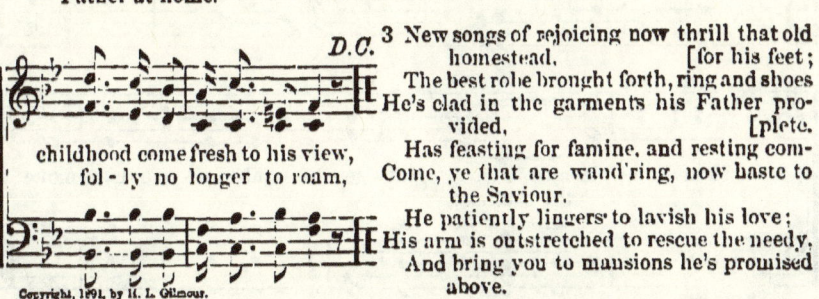

childhood come fresh to his view,
fol - ly no longer to roam,

3 New songs of rejoicing now thrill that old
    homestead,   [for his feet;
The best robe brought forth, ring and shoes
He's clad in the garments his Father pro-
    vided,   [plete.
Has feasting for famine, and resting com-
Come, ye that are wand'ring, now haste to
    the Saviour.
He patiently lingers to lavish his love;
His arm is outstretched to rescue the needy,
And bring you to mansions he's promised
    above.

Copyright, 1891, by H. L. Gilmour.

Make me a Worker for Jesus. 67

EBEN E. REXFORD.   "And every man to his work."—Mark xiii. 34.   T. C. O'KANE.

1. Make me a work-er for Je - sus, Steadfast and earnest and true;
2. Let me be brave in the con - flict, Read-y to go where he needs,
3. Let me go out to the har - vest, Faithful-ly doing my part,
4. Make me a work-er for Je - sus, Trusting him nev-er in vain,

Willing to work for the Mas-ter, What he would have me to do.
Sowing good seed for the har - vest, Plucking up bri-ars and weeds.
Gathering sheaves for the glean-ing, Steadfast of purpose and heart.
Glad if I bind for the Mas-ter Sheaves of God's beautiful grain.

CHORUS.

Make me a worker for Je - sus, Humble my la-bor may be, But
cheer-ful-ly done for the Mas-ter, Who hath done great things for me.

68. Tell it Out with Gladness.

Fanny J. Crosby.   Jno. R. Sweney.

Moderato.

1. Are you hap-py in the Lord, Tell it out with gladness; Are you trusting in his word, Tell it out with gladness; If a Saviour's love you feel, Can your soul its power conceal? To the world your joy reveal, Tell it out with gladness.

2. Are you walking in the light, Tell it out with gladness; Is your hope of glory bright, Tell it out with gladness; Have you perfect peace within, Are you try-ing still to win Constant victory o-ver sin, Tell it out with gladness.

3. Do you love the place of prayer, Tell it out with gladness; Do you find a blessing there, Tell it out with gladness; While your thoughts on Jesus dwell, Does your soul with rapture swell? Can you say that all is well? Tell it out with gladness.

CHORUS.

Tell it out, tell it out, tell it out with gladness, Tell it out, tell it out, tell it out with gladness, Tell the world . . . the joy you feel, tell the world the joy you feel, tell the

Copyright, 1889, by Jno. R. Sweney.

Tell it Out with Gladness.—CONCLUDED. 69

feel, Tell it out, tell it out with glad-ness.
world the joy you feel,

COWPER. **Glorious Fountain.** T. C. O'KANE.
By per.

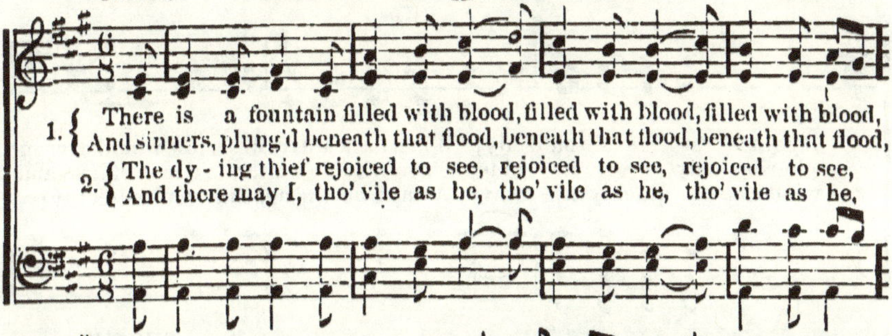

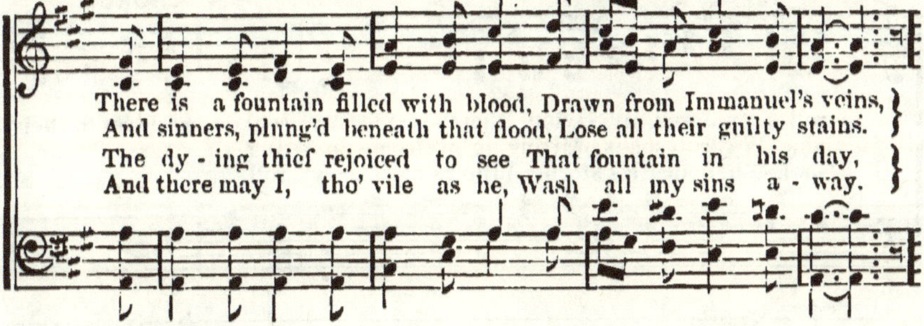

1. There is a fountain filled with blood, filled with blood, filled with blood,
   And sinners, plung'd beneath that flood, beneath that flood, beneath that flood,
2. The dy-ing thief rejoiced to see, rejoiced to see, rejoiced to see,
   And there may I, tho' vile as he, tho' vile as he, tho' vile as he,

There is a fountain filled with blood, Drawn from Immanuel's veins,
And sinners, plung'd beneath that flood, Lose all their guilty stains.
The dy-ing thief rejoiced to see That fountain in his day,
And there may I, tho' vile as he, Wash all my sins a-way.

CHORUS.

Oh, glo-ri-ous fountain! Here will I stay, And in thee ev-er
Wash my sins a-way.

3 Thou dying Lamb, ‖: thy precious blood :‖
Shall never lose its power,
Till all the ransomed ‖: Church of God :‖
Are saved, to sin no more.

4 E'er since by faith ‖: I saw the stream :‖
Thy flowing wounds supply,
Redeeming love ‖: has been my theme, :‖
And shall be till I die.

As Doves to their, etc.—CONCLUDED.

I thirst, Thou wounded Lamb.

NICOLAUS L. ZINZENDORF. Chorus added.   JNO. R. SWENEY.

1. I thirst, thou wounded Lamb of God, To wash me in thy cleansing blood;
2. Take my poor heart, and let it be For-ev-er closed to all but thee:
3. How blest are they who still abide Close sheltered in thy bleeding side!
4. What are our works but sin and death, Till thou thy quickening Spirit breathe?

To dwell within thy wounds; then pain Is sweet, and life or death is gain.
Seal thou my breast, and let me wear That pledge of love for-ev-er there.
Who thence their life and strength derive, And by thee move, and in thee live.
Thou giv'st the power thy grace to move; O wondrous grace! O wondrous love!

D.S.—let my soul remain, For life or death with thee is gain.

CHORUS.

I trust in thy redeeming blood, O wash me in the precious flood; Here, Saviour,

Copyright, 1893, by Jno. R. Sweney.

5 How can it be, thou heavenly King,
That thou shouldst us to glory bring?
Make slaves the partners of thy throne,
Decked with a never-fading crown?

6 Hence our hearts melt, our eyes o'erflow,
Our words are lost, nor will we know,
Nor will we think of aught beside,
"My Lord, my Love is crucified."

Throw Out the Life-Line. 73

(May be sung as a Solo and Chorus.)

Rev. E. S. Ufford.   E. S. U. Arr. by Geo. C. Stebbins.

1. Throw out the life-line a-cross the dark wave, There is a brother whom some one should save; Somebod-y's brother! oh, who then, will dare To throw out the life-line, his per-il to share? Throw out the life-line!
2. Throw out the life-line with hand quick and strong: Why do you tarry, why lin-ger so long? See! he is sinking, oh, hast-en to day—And out with the life-boat! a-way, then, a-way
3. Throw out the life-line to danger-fraught men, Sinking in anguish where you've nev-er been: Winds of temptation and bil-lows of woe Will soon hurl them out where the dark waters flow.
4. Soon will the season of res-cue be o'er, Soon will they drift to e-ter-ni-ty's shore, Haste then, my brother, no time for de-lay, But throw out the life-line, and save them to-day.

CHORUS.

Throw out the life-line! Some one is drifting a-way; Throw out the life-line! Throw out the life-line! Some one is sinking to-day.

Copyright, 1890, by The Biglow & Main Co. Used by permission.

74. "This I Did for Thee."

H. BONAR.   W. H. DOANE.

Slow.

1. I gave my life for thee, My precious blood I shed, That thou might'st ransom'd be,
2. I spent long years for thee In weariness and woe, That one e-ter-ni-ty
3. My Father's house of light, My rainbow-circled throne, I left for earthly night,
4. I suffered much for thee,—More than my tongue can tell, Of bitterest agony;

And quickened from the dead; I gave my life for thee; What hast thou done for me?
Of joy thou mightest know; I spent long years for thee; Hast thou spent one for me?
For wand'rings sad and lone; I left it all all for thee; Hast thou left aught for me?
To rescue thee from hell; I suffered much for thee; What dost thou bear for me?

CHORUS.

This I did for thee,   What hast thou done for me?
This I did for thee, What hast thou done for me? Yes,

This I did for thee,   What hast thou done for me?
this I did for thee,

5 And I have brought to thee,
   Down from my house above,
   Salvation full and free,
   My pardon and my love;
   Great gifts I brought to thee;
   What hast thou brought to me?

6 Oh, let thy life be given,
   Thy years for me be spent,
   World fetters all be riven,
   And joy with suffering blent;
   Give thou thyself to me,
   And I will welcome thee!

Used by permission of with W. H. Doane, owner of Copyright.

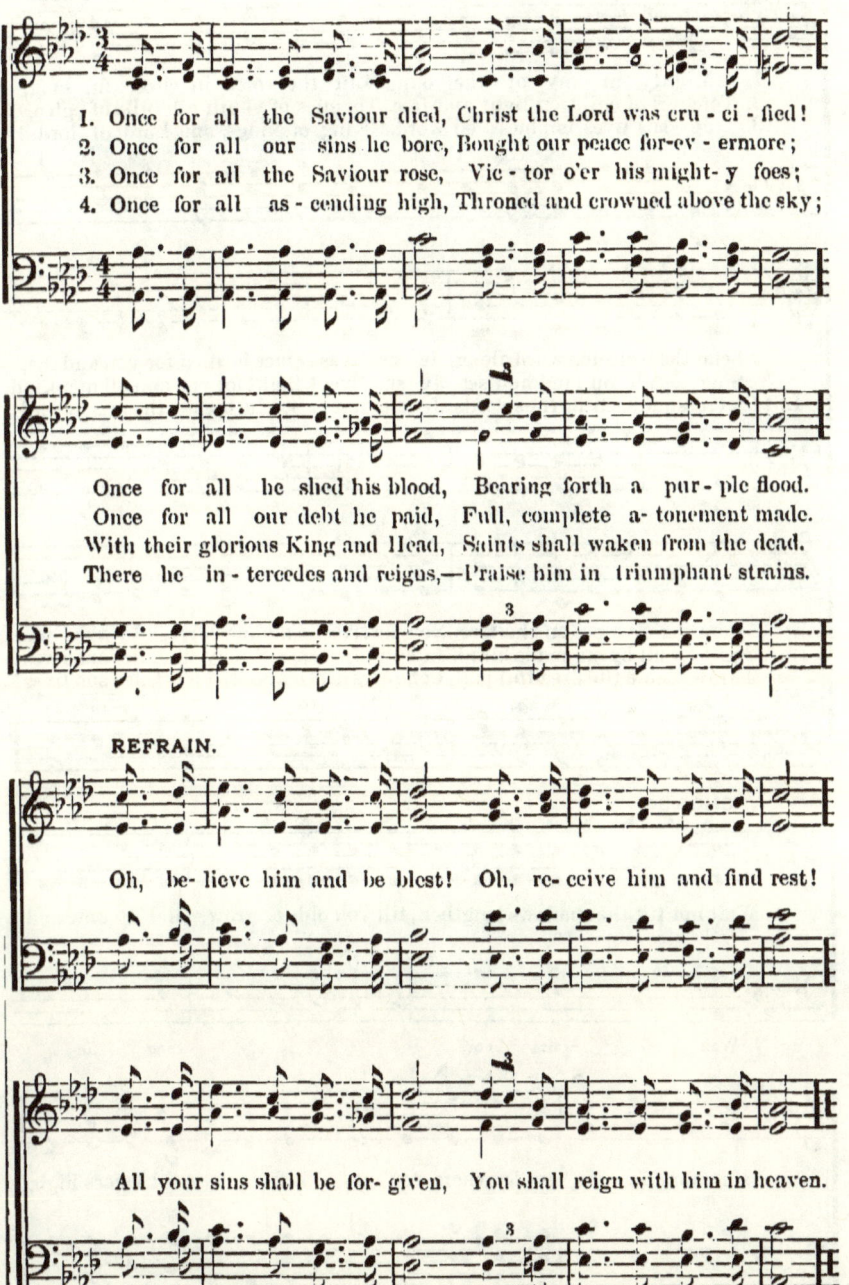

Jesus Lives! —CONCLUDED.

Repeat chorus pp.
f rit.

Ringing clear thro' earth and sky, Let the blessed tidings fly, Je- sus lives!

Rest, weary Heart.

L. H. EDMUNDS.   JNO. R. SWENEY.

1. Rest, weary heart, For Je-sus bids thee rest; Sweet comfort find Up-
2. Come, with thy fears, With all thy griefs to-day; His gen- tle hand Will
3. Tell him thy need, Yea, o - pen all thy heart; His mighty love Will
4. Rest, weary heart, Upon thy heavenly Friend; Till morning break, And

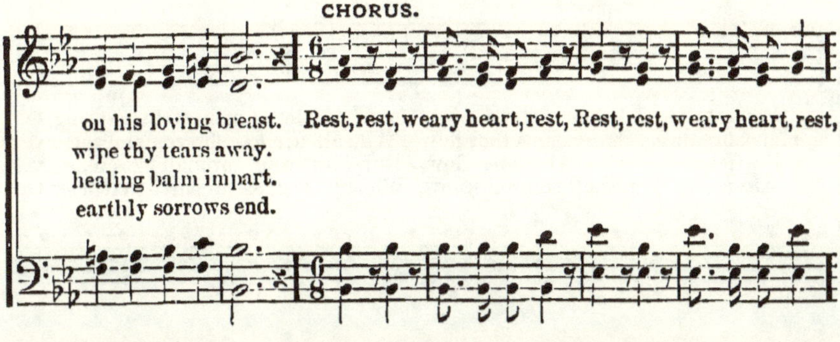

CHORUS.

on his loving breast.   Rest, rest, weary heart, rest, Rest, rest, weary heart, rest,
wipe thy tears away.
healing balm impart.
earthly sorrows end.

And find sweet comfort, find sweet comfort, find sweet comfort On thy Saviour's breast.

Copyright, 1882, by Jno. R. Sweney.

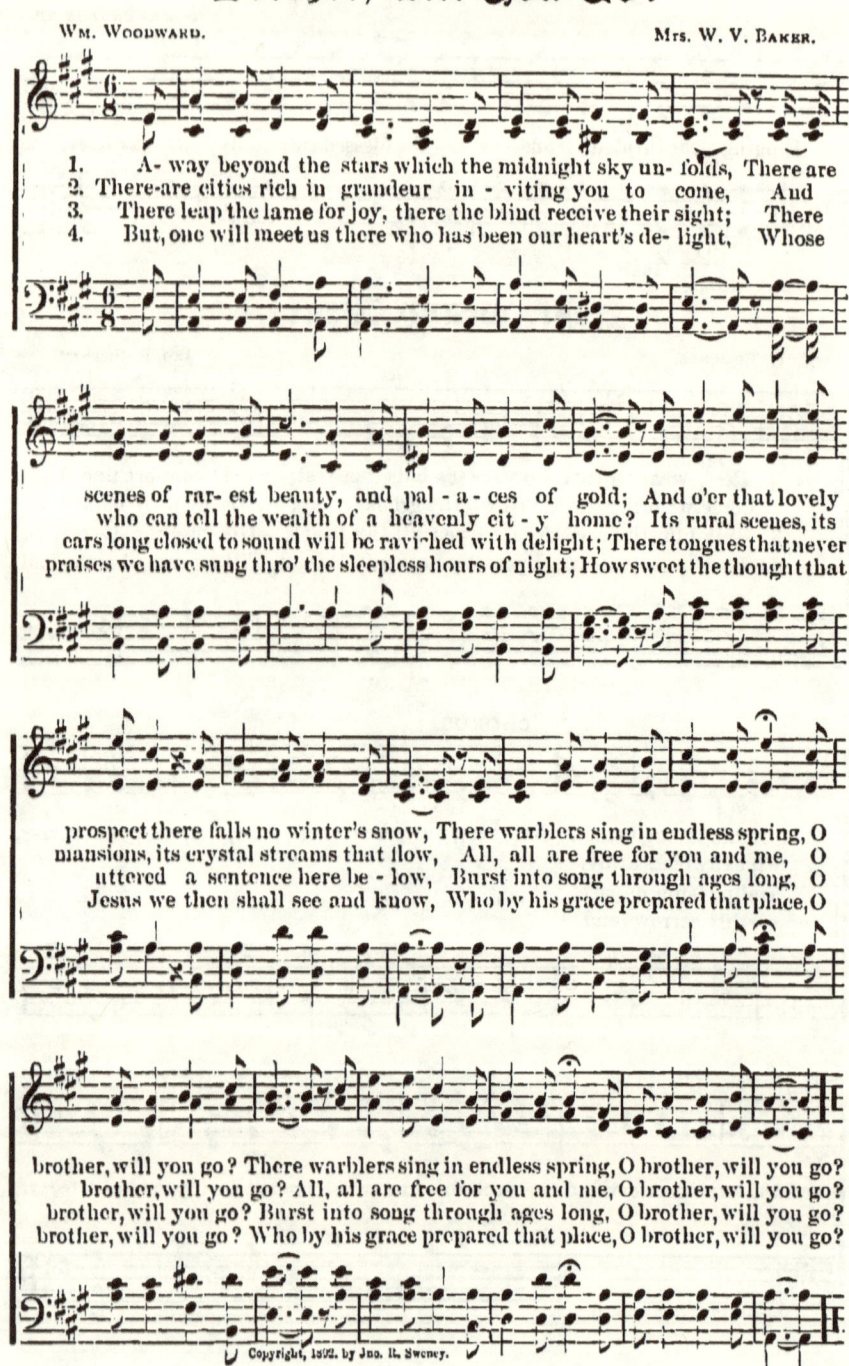

The World is my Parish.

From the "Singing Pilgrim."   T. C. O'Kane. By per.

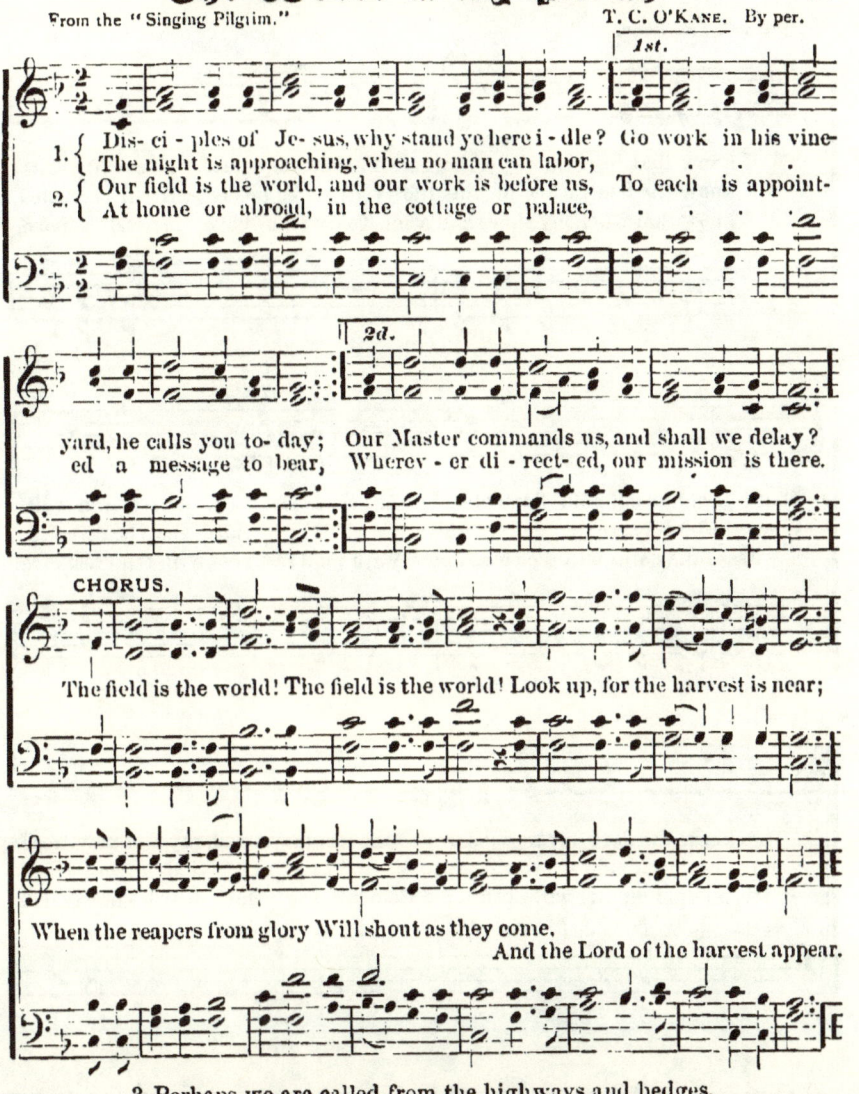

3 Perhaps we are called from the highways and hedges,
  To gather the lowly, despised, and oppressed;
  If this be our duty, then why should we falter?
  We'll do it, and trust to our Saviour the rest.

4 O'er islands that sleep in the wave-crested ocean,
  We'll scatter the truth, and its fruit it shall bear;
  O'er ice-covered regions and rock-girded mountains
  The Lord will protect as his children are there.

5 Instead of the thorn shall the myrtle be planted;
  The desert shall blossom and bloom as the rose;
  The palm-tree rejoicing shall spread forth her branch
  The lamb and the lion together repose.

80. So I Can Wait.

JULIA C. THOMPSON. JNO. R. SWENEY.

1. I know that heav'n lies just beyond This earthly state, this earthly state;
2. I know the heartaches of this life Will all be healed, will all be healed,
3. I know that when my time shall come To dwell a-bove, to dwell a-bove,

That Christ himself holds death's cold wand; So I can wait, so I can wait.
When the blest peace that ends earth's strife Shall be revealed, shall be revealed.
Jesus his child will welcome home With tend'rest love, with tend'rest love.

I know the dark, mysterious ways My feet may tread, my feet may tread
I know that 'mid the world's turmoil God giveth rest, God giveth rest;
His an-gel guards will open wide Heav'n's pearly gate, heav'n's pearly gate;

Will all be plain when heav'nly rays Are on them shed, are on them shed.
His arm is round me in its toil And I am blest, and I am blest.
And I shall then be *sat-is-fied:* So I can wait, so I can wait!

Copyright, 1878, by Jno. R. Sweney.

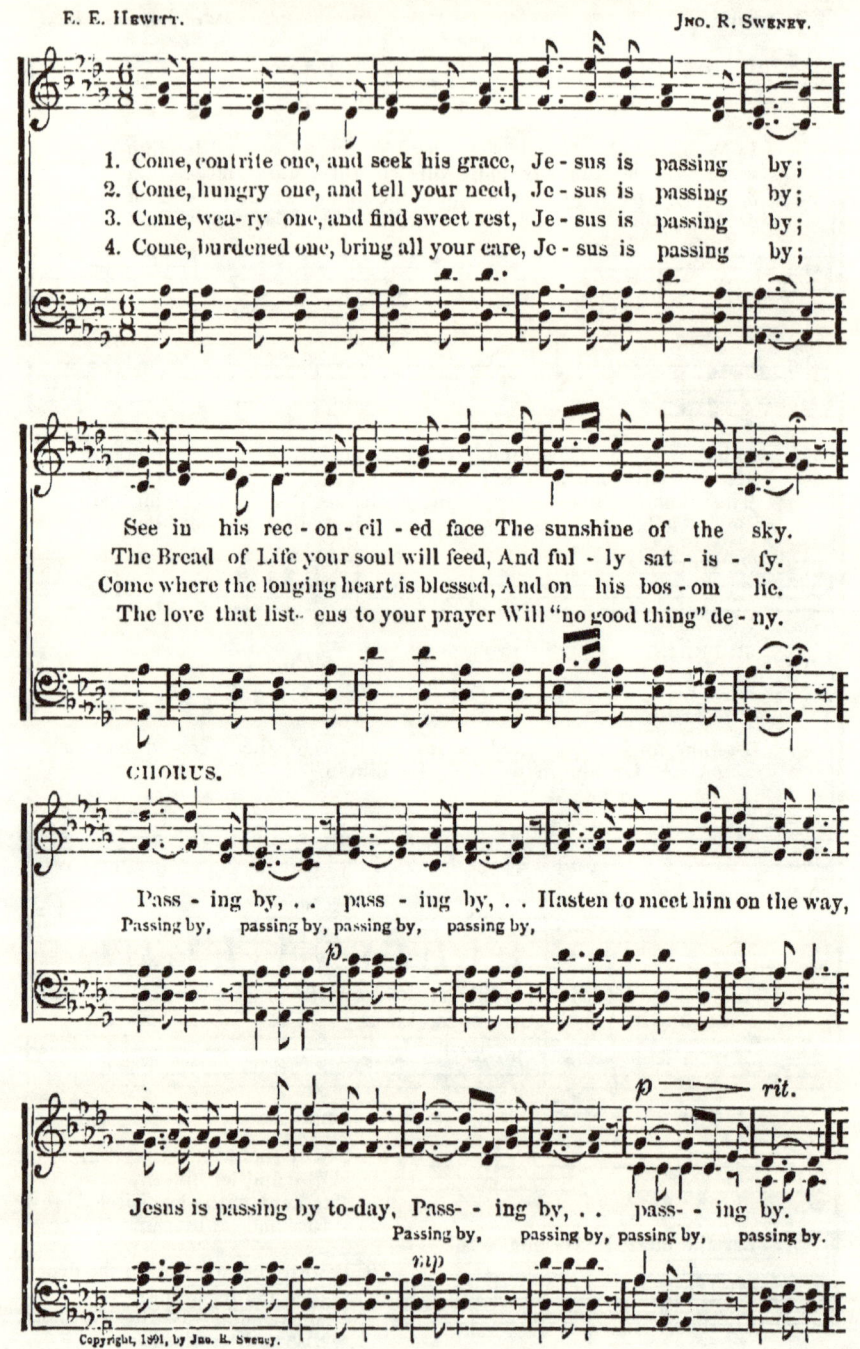

A Shelter in the Time of Storm. 83

"God is the rock of my refuge."—Ps. xciv: 22.

Words arranged. A J. Showalter. By per.

1. The Lord's our Rock, in him we hide, A shelter in the time of storm;
2. A shade by day, defence by night. A shelter in the time of storm;
3. The raging storms may round us beat, A shelter in the time of storm;
4. O Rock divine, O Refuge dear, A shelter in the time of storm;

Se-cure whatev-er may be-tide, A shelter in the time of storm.
No fears a-larm, no foes affright, A shelter in the time of storm.
We'll nev-er leave this safe retreat, A shelter in the time of storm.
Be thou our helper ev-er near, A shelter in the time of storm.

CHORUS.

Oh, Jesus is a Rock in a weary land, A weary land, a weary land;

Jesus is a Rock in a weary land, A shelter in the time of storm.

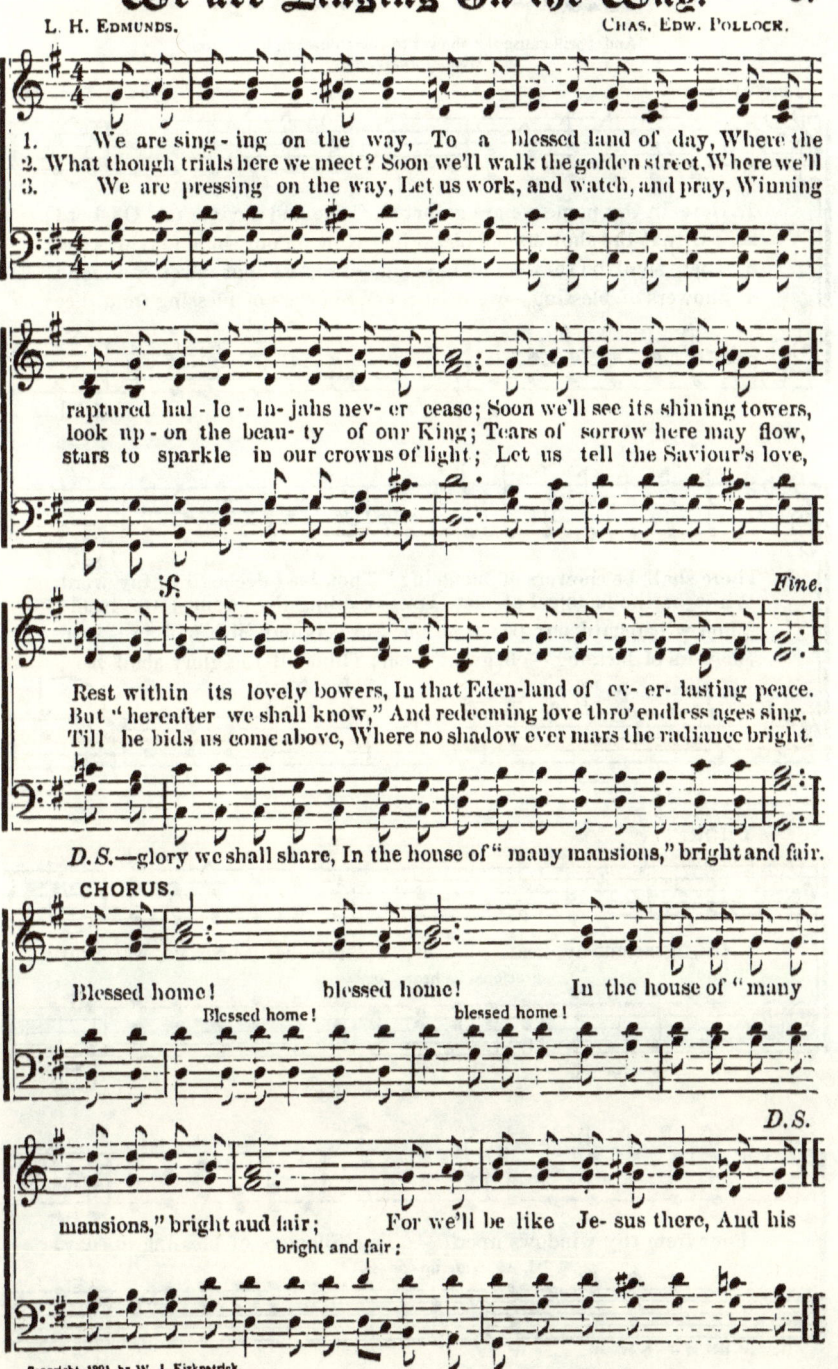

A Blessing in Prayer. 91

E. E. Hewitt. Wm. J. Kirkpatrick.

1. There is rest, sweet rest, at the Master's feet, There is favor now at the mer-cy seat, For a-ton-ing blood has been sprinkled there; There is
2. There is grace to help in our time of need, For our friend above is a friend in-deed, We may cast on him ev-'ry grief and care; There is
3. When our songs are glad with the joy of life, When our hearts are sad with its ills and strife, When the powers of sin would the soul ensnare, There is
4. There is perfect peace though the wild waves roll; There are gifts of love for the seek-ing soul; Till we praise the Lord in his home so fair, There is

REFRAIN.

always a blessing, a blessing in prayer. There's a blessing in prayer, in be-lieving prayer; When our Saviour's name to the throne we bear, Then a Father's love will receive us there; There is always a blessing, a blessing in prayer.

Copyright, 1887, by Wm. J. Kirkpatrick.

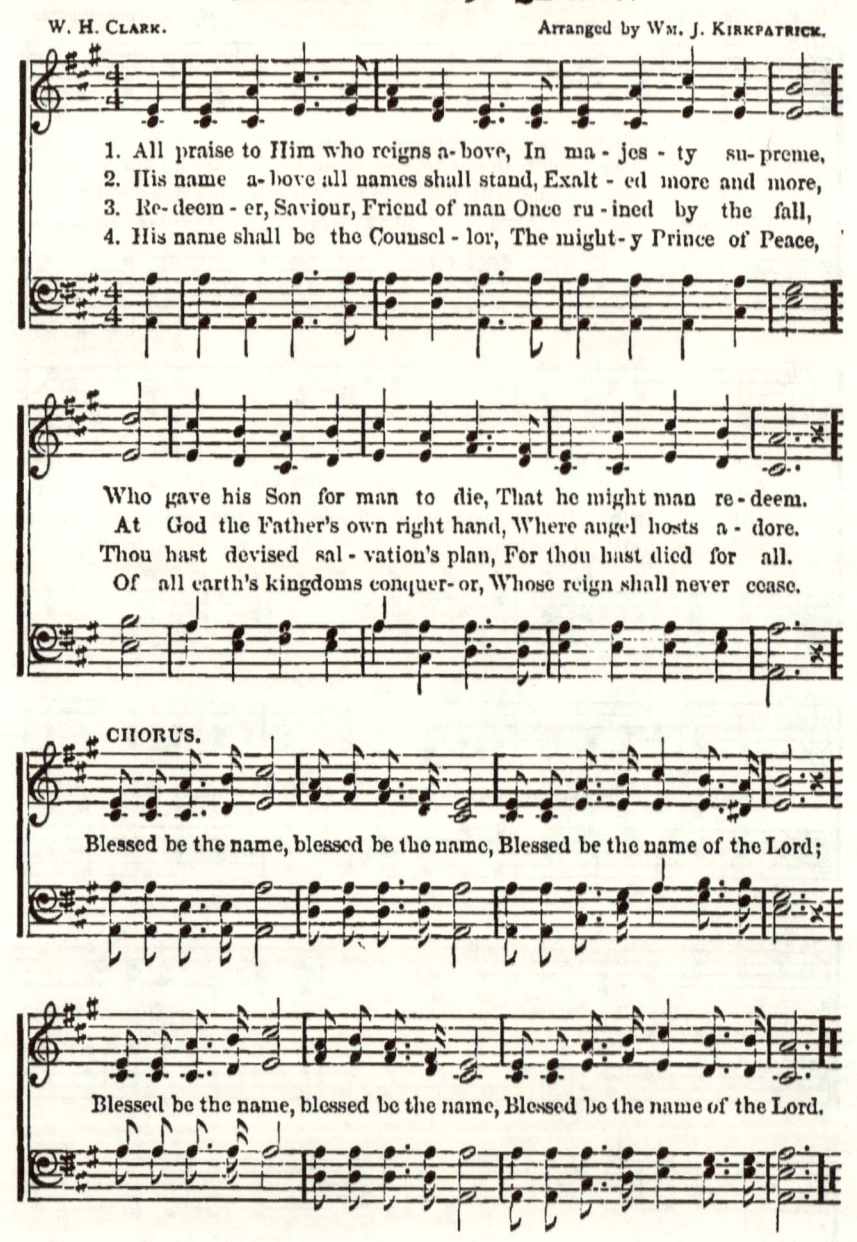

Only Believe.

Emma M. Johnston. Mark v. 36. Wm. J. Kirkpatrick.

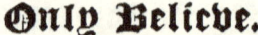

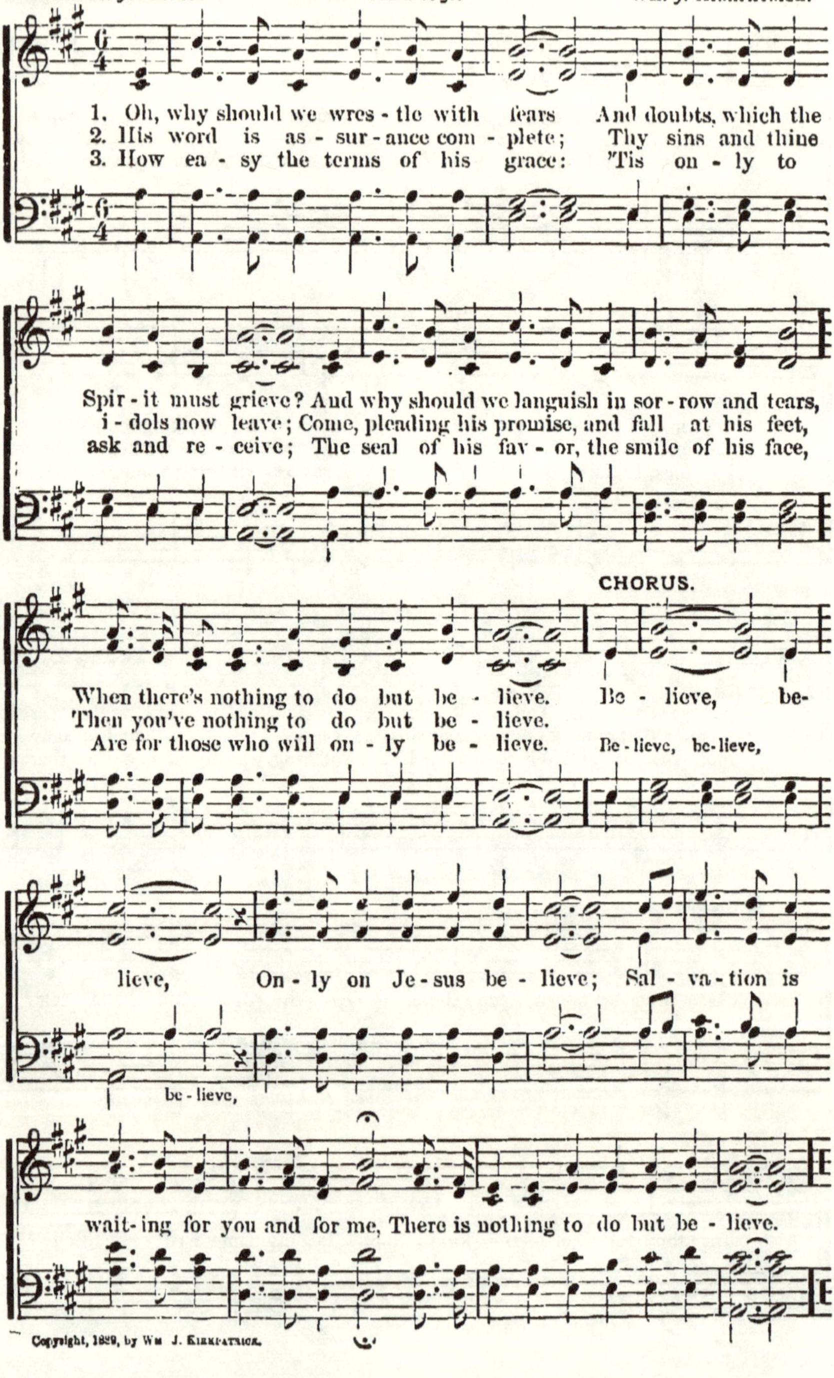

100. Do Something To-Day.

LANTA WILSON SMITH. WM. J. KIRKPATRICK.

1. You're longing to work for the Master, Yet waiting for something to do;
2. Go rescue that wandering brother Who sinks 'neath his burden of woe,
3. Go sing happy songs of rejoicing With those who no sorrows have known;
4. O never, my brother, stand waiting, Be willing to do what you can;

You fancy the future is holding Some wonderful mission for you;
A single kind action may save him, If love and compassion you show;
Go weep with the heart-broken mourner, Go comfort the sad and the lone;
The humblest service is need-ed, To fill out the Father's great plan;

But while you are waiting the moments Are rapid-ly passing a-way;
Don't shrink from the vilest about you, If you can but lead them from sin;
From pitfalls and snares of the tempter Go rescue the thoughtless and wild:
Be earning your stars of rejoic-ing While earth-life is passing a-way;

O brother, awake from your dreaming, Do something for Jesus to-day.
For this is the grandest of missions,— Lost souls for the Master to win.
Go win from pale lips a 'God bless you,' Go brighten the life of a child.
Win some one to meet you in glo-ry,— Do something for Jesus to-day.

Copyright, 1888, by Wm. J. Kirkpatrick

Do Something To=Day. — CONCLUDED

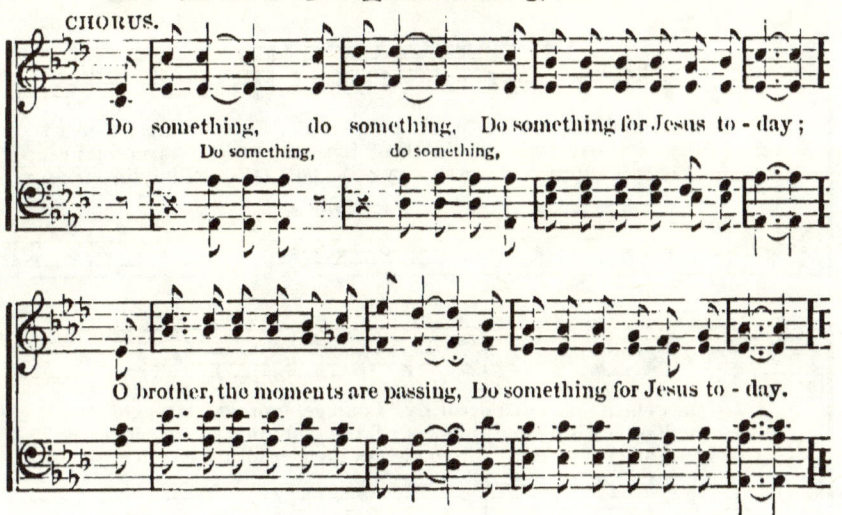

Jesus will Meet You There.

W. L. K. W. Lewis Kane.

2 Rest beneath the hallowed cross,
  Jesus will meet you there;
  Saving mercy gained for loss,
  Jesus will meet you there.

3 Come and join his faithful band,
  Jesus will meet you there;
  Take his mighty, helping hand,
  Jesus will meet you there.

4 At the blessed mercy seat,
  Jesus will meet you there;
  Come with this assurance sweet,
  Jesus will meet you there.

5 You'll find rest in heaven at last,
  Jesus will meet you there;
  And be happy with the blest,
  Jesus will meet you there.

Copyright, 1886, by Jno. R. Sweney.

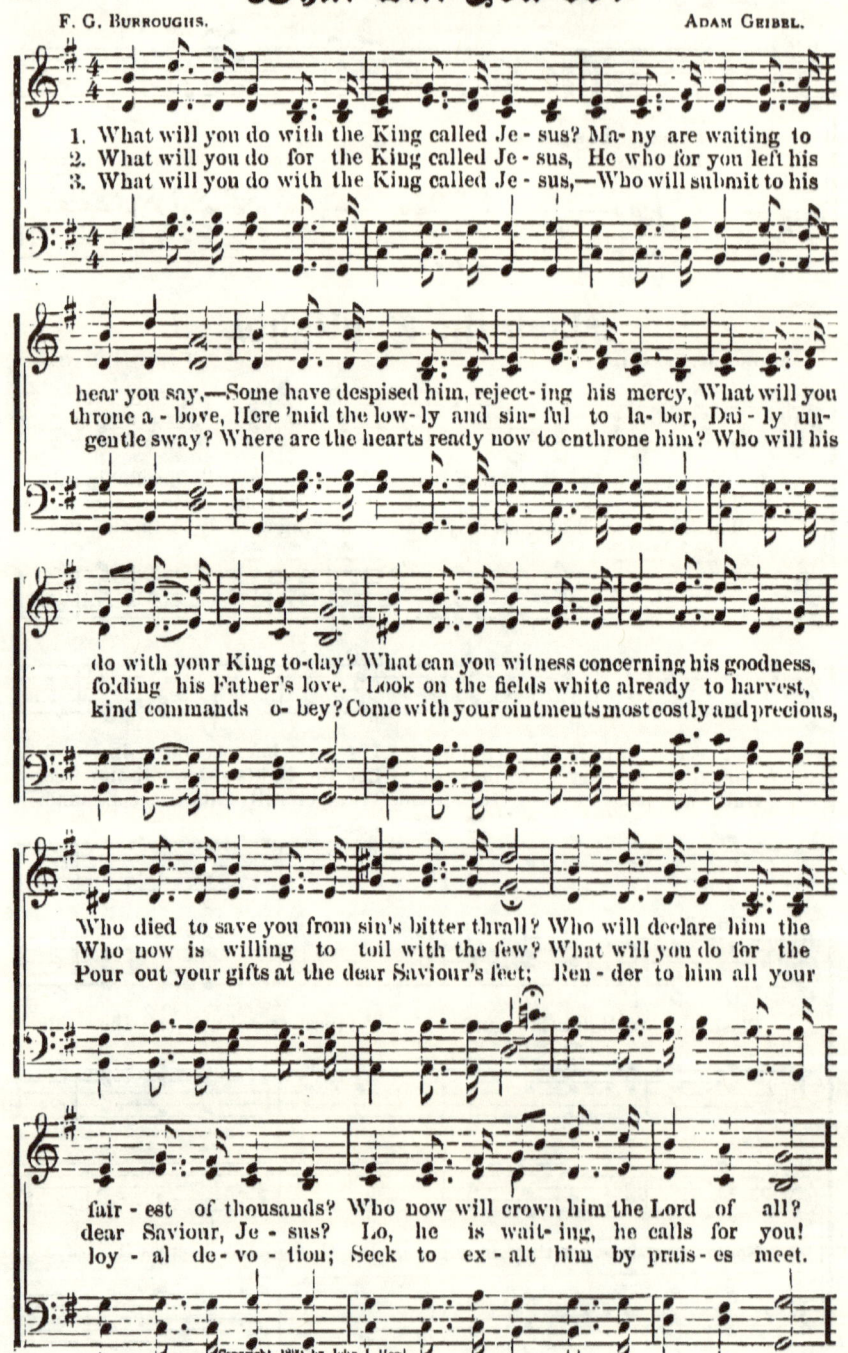

2 One more soul is redeemed from sin,
 Washed in the blood of the Lamb;
One more heart that was tossed within,
 Now has perpetual calm.

3 Help us, Saviour, the vict'ry gain,
 Under thy banner of love;
Ever, then, shall we praise thy name,
 And dwell with thee above.

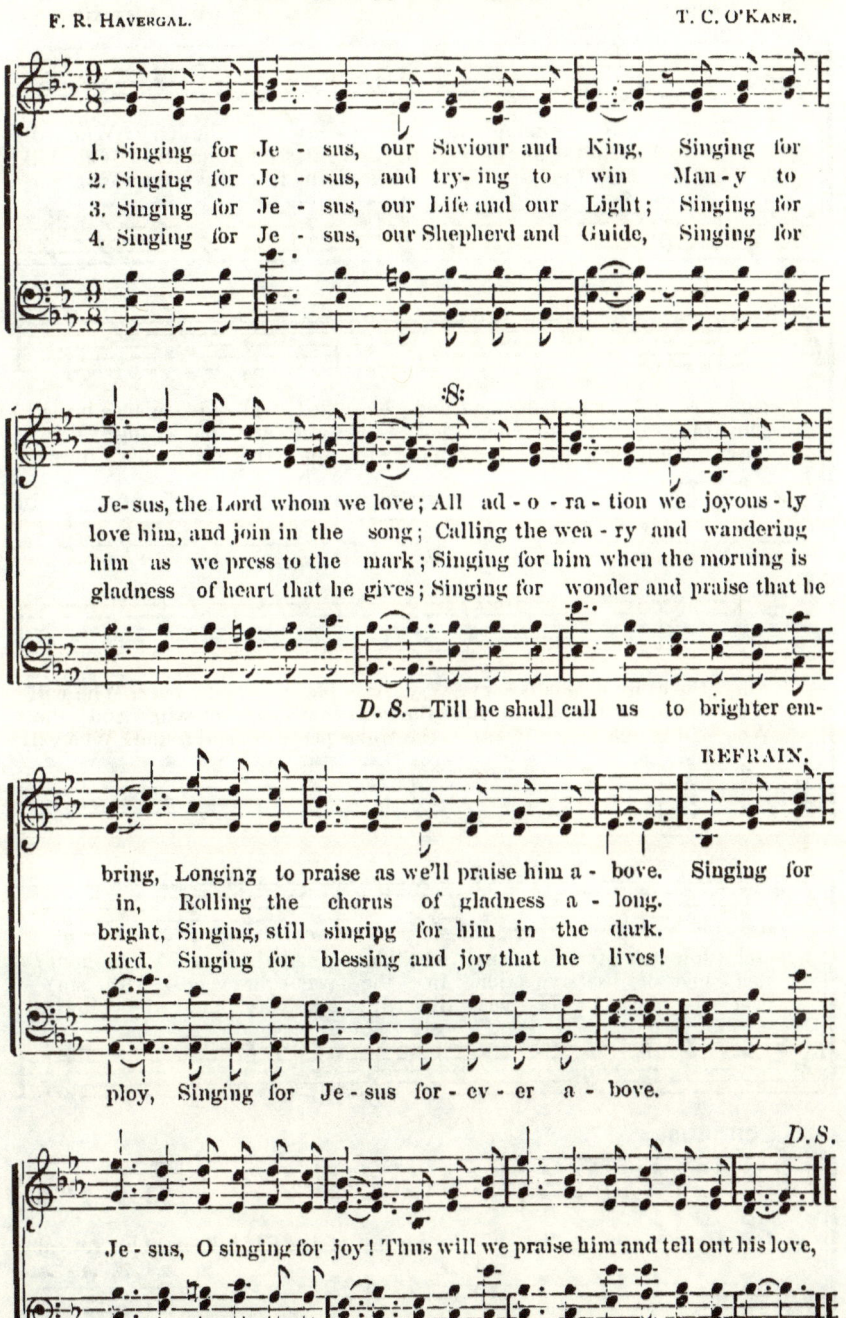

108. Put My Name On the List.

E. E. Hewitt.   Wm. J. Kirkpatrick.

1. Who'll en-roll his name in the ar-my of the King? Who will sign a life-en-list-ment, and his full al-le-giance bring? For the cause demands ev-'ry no-ble gift and power; Who will fol-low af-ter Je-sus? who'll be-gin this ver-y hour?
2. Who will wield the sword of the Spir-it, strong and true? Who will join the roy-al ar-my, and the Lead-er's bid-ing do? Who will take the shield of the faith that's sure to win, And the "hel-met of sal-va-tion," in the war-fare waged with sin?
3. Who are on the side of the good, the true, the pure? Who will raise the might-y stand-ard? Who will to the end en-dure? Who will march or halt, as the trum-pet-call shall sound? Who will bear the cross for Je-sus, till with star-ry light he's crowned?

CHORUS.

Put my name on the list of the ar-my of the King, To fight his roy-al

Copyright, 1891, by Wm. J. Kirkpatrick.

4 Pass me not, O mighty Spirit!
   Thou can'st make the blind to see;
   Witnesser of Jesus' merit,
   Speak the word of power to me,—
      Even me, even me, etc.

5 Love of God, so pure and changeless;
   Blood of Christ, so rich and free;
   Grace of God, so strong and boundless,
   Magnify them all in me,—
      Even me, even me, etc.

Send the Light.—CONCLUDED.

Send the light, ... the bless-ed gos-pel light,
Send the light! . . . . . and let its ra-diant beams

Let it shine . . . . from shore to shore! . . . . . .
Light the world . . . for-ev-er - - - - - - more, ...
          for-ev-ermore.

Praise, Praise His Name.

FANNY J. CROSBY. JNO. R. SWENEY.

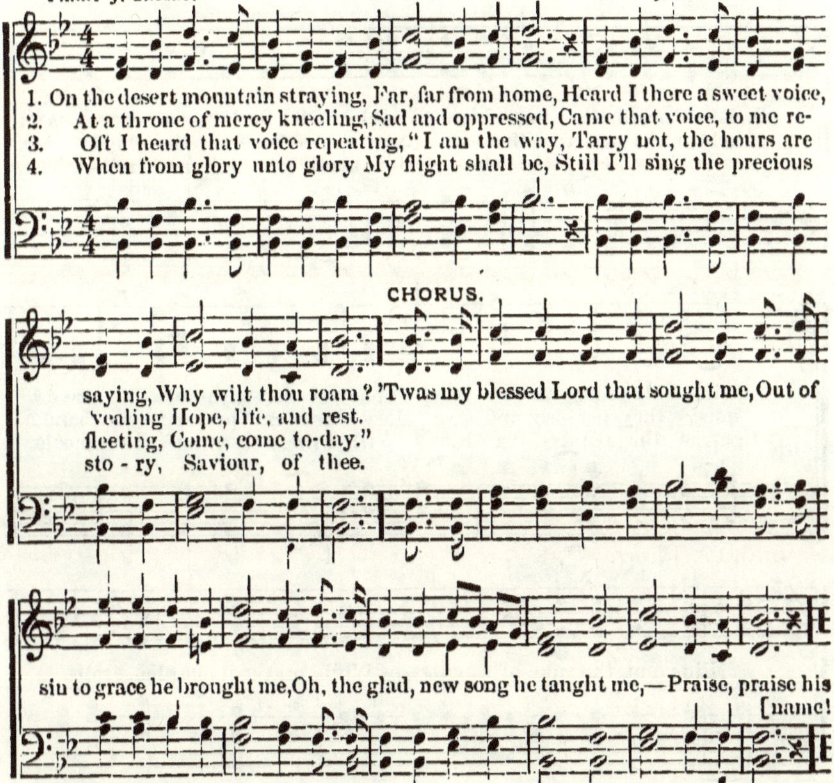

1. On the desert mountain straying, Far, far from home, Heard I there a sweet voice,
2. At a throne of mercy kneeling, Sad and oppressed, Came that voice, to me re-
3. Oft I heard that voice repeating, "I am the way, Tarry not, the hours are
4. When from glory unto glory My flight shall be, Still I'll sing the precious

CHORUS.

saying, Why wilt thou roam? 'Twas my blessed Lord that sought me, Out of
vealing Hope, life, and rest.
fleeting, Come, come to-day."
sto-ry, Saviour, of thee.

sin to grace he brought me, Oh, the glad, new song he taught me,—Praise, praise his
[name!

Copyright, 1891, by John R. Sweney.

On the Shoals.—CONCLUDED.

That he who rules the storm.... Will bring them off the shoals.

Step Out on the Promise.

Maggie Potter. Arr. by E. F. M. E. F. Miller.

1. O mourner in Zi-on, how blessed art thou, For Je-sus is waiting to com-fort thee now, Fear not to re-ly on the word of thy God; Step out on the promise,—get under the blood.
2. O ye that are hun-gry and thirsty, re-joice! For ye shall be filled; do you hear that sweet voice In-vit-ing you now to the ban-quet of God? Step out on the promise,—get under the blood.
3. Who sighs for a heart from in-i-qui-ty free? O poor, troubled soul! there's a promise for thee, There's rest, weary one, in the bos-om of God; Step out on the promise,—get under the blood.
4. Step out on the promise, and Christ you shall win, "The blood of his Son cleanseth us from all sin," It cleanseth me now, hal-le-lu-jah to God! I rest on his promise,—I'm under the blood.

From "The Shout of Victory," by per.

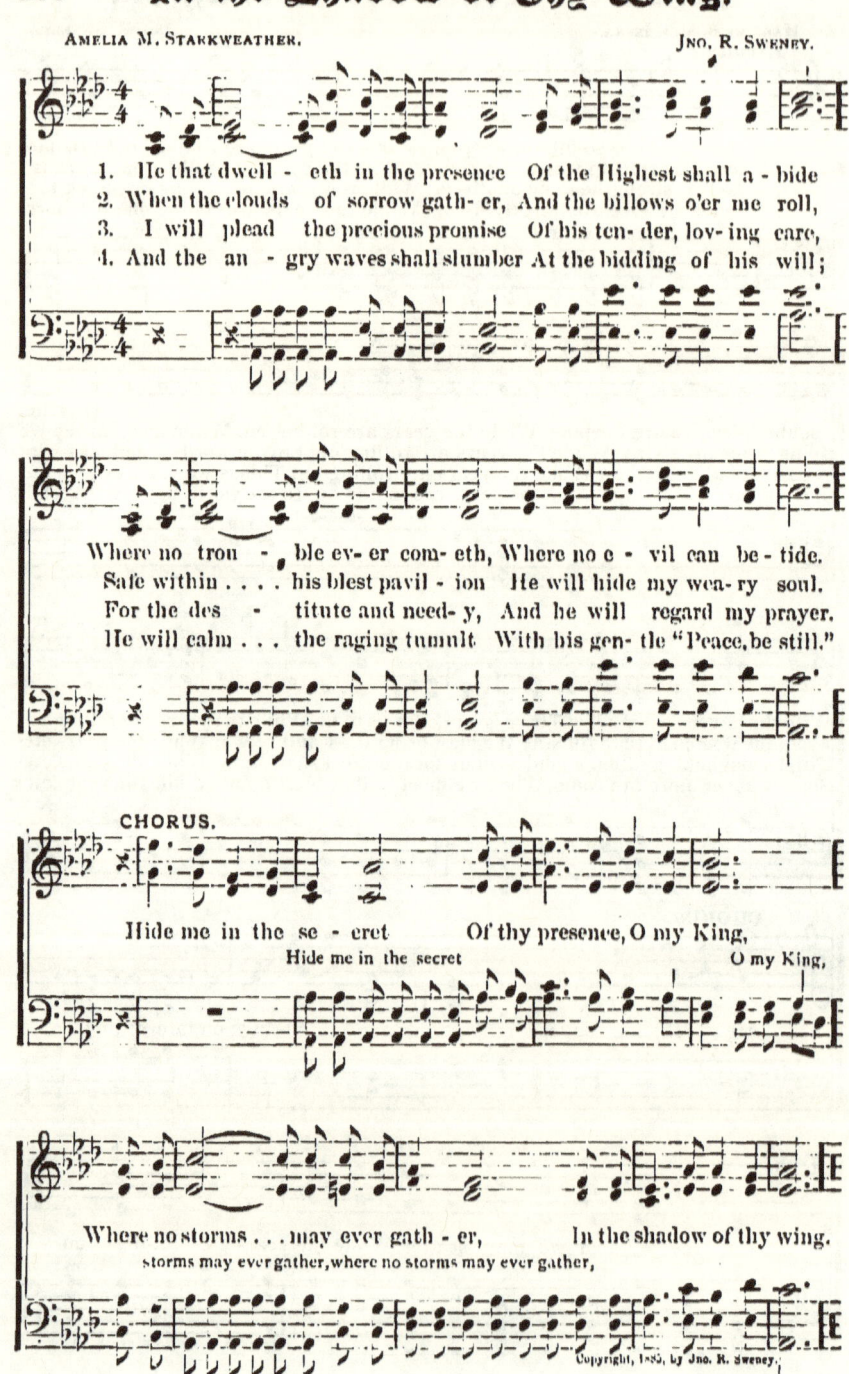

How can I Keep from Singing?   117

"The redeemed of the Lord shall return, and come with singing unto Zion; and everlasting joy shall be upon their head."—Is. li: 11.

R. I. Rev. R. Lowry. By per.

1. My life flows on in endless song; Above earth's lamen - ta - tion
2. What tho' my joys and comforts die? The Lord my Saviour liv- eth!
3. I lift my eyes; the cloud grows thin, I see the blue a - bove it;

I catch the sweet, tho' far- off hymn That hails a new cre - a - tion;
What tho' the darkness gather round? Songs in the night he giv - eth:
And day by day this pathway smooths, Since first I learned to love it:

Thro' all the tu - mult and the strife I hear the mu - sic ringing;
No storm can shake my inmost calm, While to that ref - uge clinging;
The peace of Christ makes fresh my heart, A fountain ev - er springing;

It finds an ech - o in my soul—How can I keep from singing?
Since Christ is Lord of heav'n and earth, How can I keep from singing?
All things are mine since I am his—How can I keep from singing?

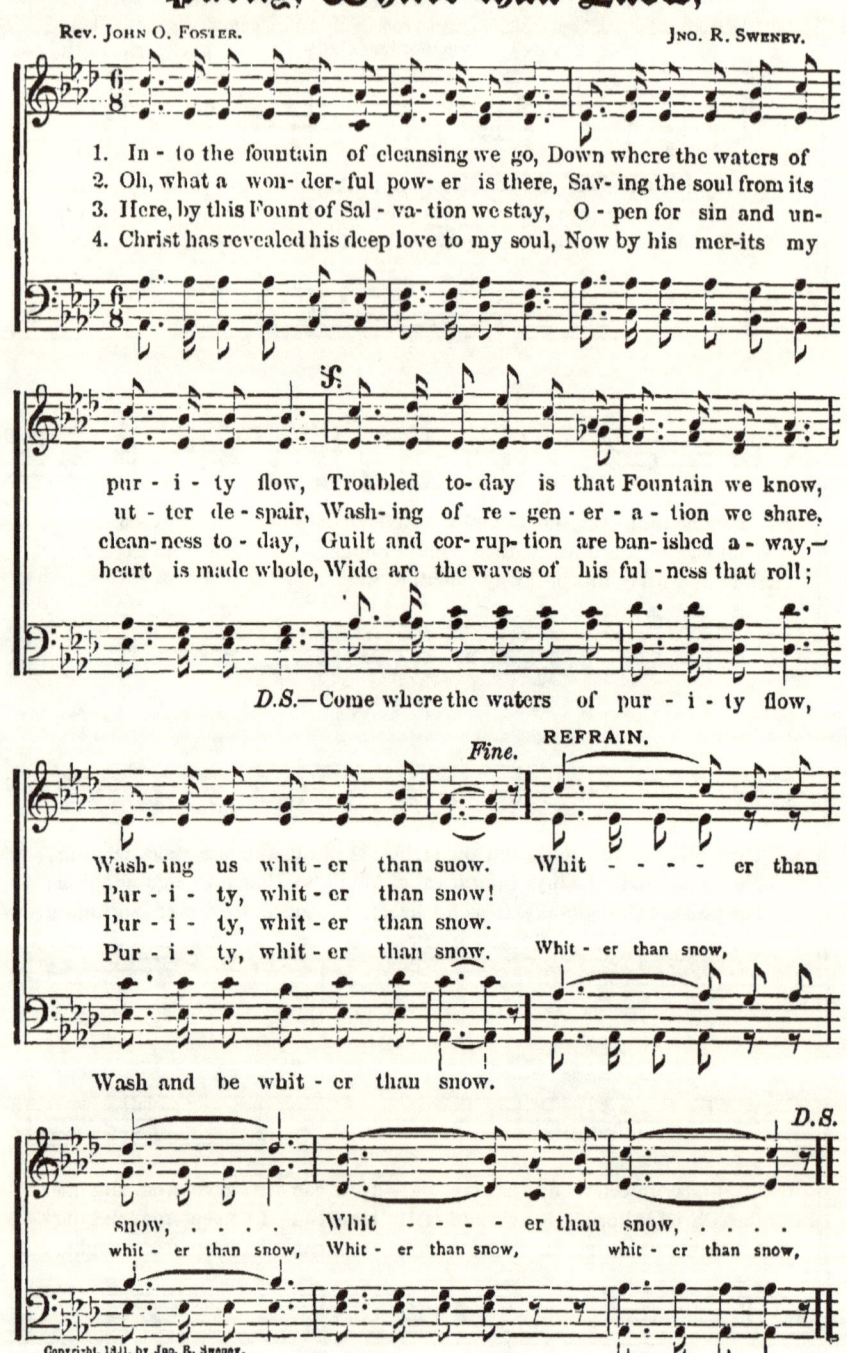

In the Shadow of the Cross. 119

"God forbid that I should glory, save in the cross of our Lord Jesus Christ."—Gal. vi : 14.

E. R. LATTA.   J. H. TENNEY. By per.

1. There's a place a - bove all others, Where my spir- it loves to be;
2. On the cross my Saviour suffered That he might a- tone for me;
3. When my heart is full of trouble, Then I love, on bended knee,
4. Blessed Sa- viour, thou wilt hear me, When I make my earnest plea,

'Tis with - in the sa - cred shadow Of the cross of Cal - va - ry.
And I love the bless- ed shadow Of the cross of Cal - va - ry.
To approach him in the shadow Of the cross of Cal - va - ry.
If I kneel with - in the shadow Of the cross of Cal - va - ry.

CHORUS.

In the shadow of the cross, In the shadow of the cross;
        of the cross,   of the cross;

There my spir- it loves to be, In the shadow of the cross.

Copyright, 1883, by J. H. Tenney.

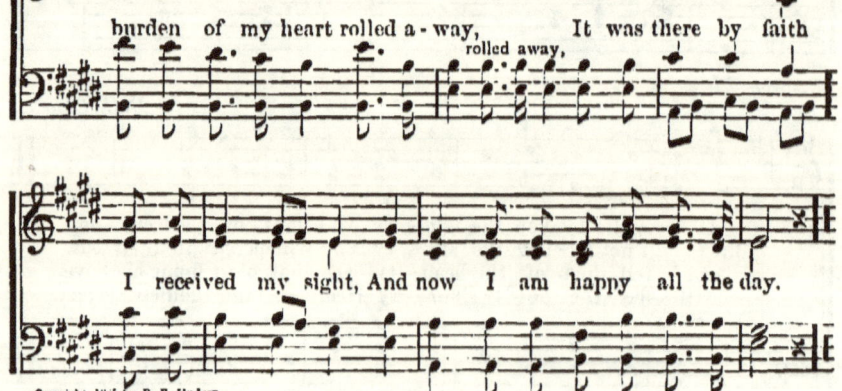

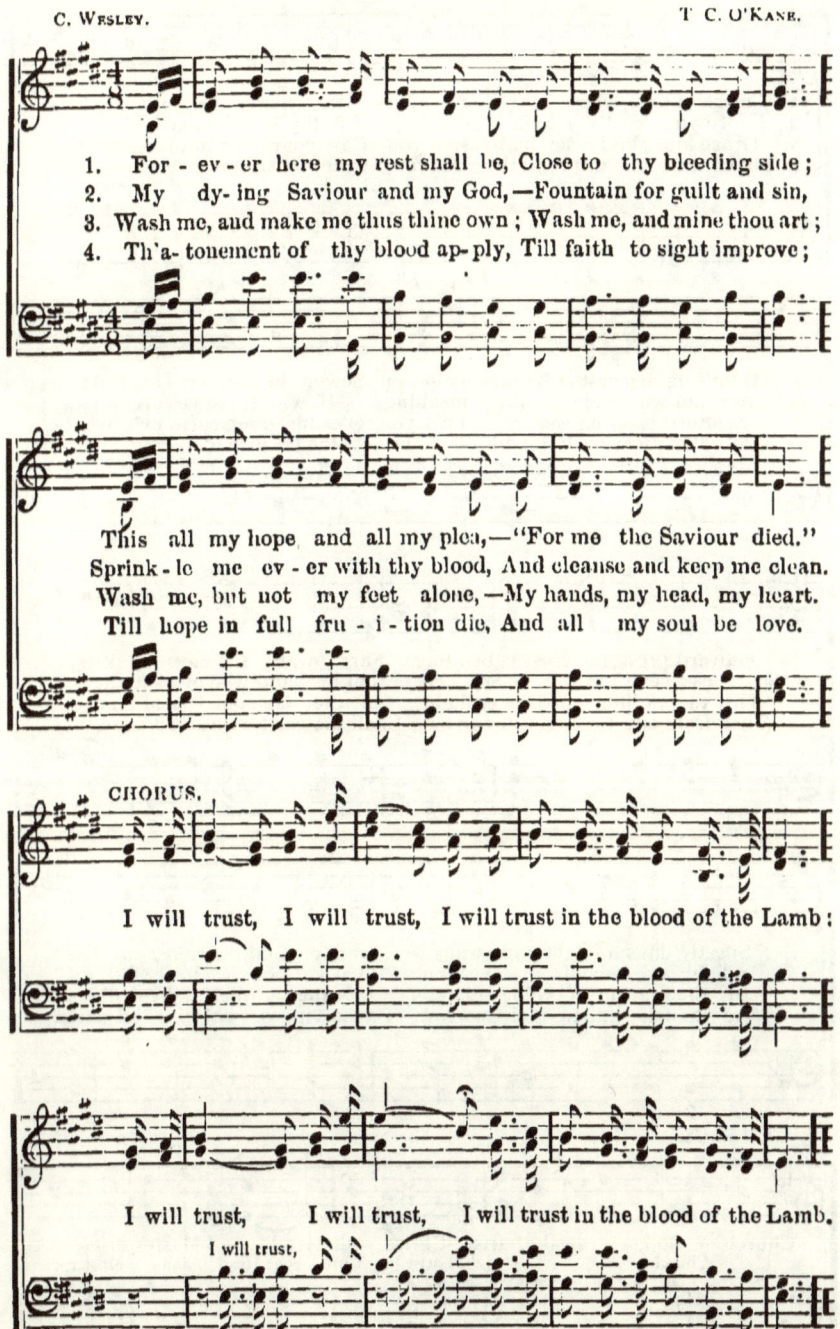

Church of God, Awake.—CONCLUDED. 125

Send the gos - pel's joyful sound Unto earth's remot- est bound.
Oh, send the gos - pel's joy- ful sound

Use Me, Saviour.

FRED. WOODROW. CHAS. H. GABRIEL.

1. Use me, O my gracious Sa- viour, Use me, Lord, as pleaseth thee;
2. Be it noon or be it midnight, Wea- ry watch or blaze of day,
3. Pride of will and lust of sta - tion, Lord, I would from all be free,

Nothing done for thee so low - ly But is great enough for me.
Shouting with the hap- py reap- ers, Toil- ing in the hidden way.
And the on - ly hon- or seek- ing, Lord, to be of use to thee.

CHORUS.

Use me, Use me, Use me as it pleaseth thee;
Use me, O my Saviour, Use me, O my Sa- viour,

Use me, Use me, Use me as it pleaseth thee.
Use me, O my Saviour, Use me, O my Saviour,

Copyright, 1891, by John J. Hood.

There is Peace in My Heart.

E. T. O'Kane.

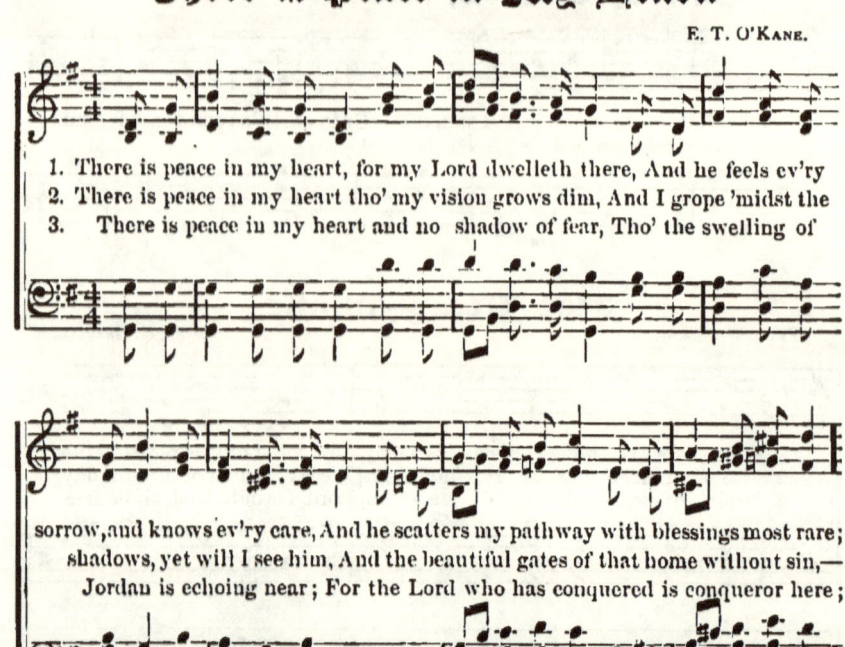

1. There is peace in my heart, for my Lord dwelleth there, And he feels ev'ry
2. There is peace in my heart tho' my vision grows dim, And I grope 'midst the
3. There is peace in my heart and no shadow of fear, Tho' the swelling of

sorrow, and knows ev'ry care, And he scatters my pathway with blessings most rare;
shadows, yet will I see him, And the beautiful gates of that home without sin,—
Jordan is echoing near; For the Lord who has conquered is conqueror here;

REFRAIN.

There is peace in my heart, for my Lord dwelleth there. There is peace in my
There is peace in my heart, for my Lord dwells within.
There is peace in my heart, for my Lord dwelleth there.

heart, restful peace, There is peace in my heart, for my Lord dwelleth there.
There is

Copyright, 1891, by T. C. O'Kane.

Jesus will Welcome Me There. 131

Fanny J. Crosby. Jno. R. Sweney.

1. Over the riv-er they call me, Friends that are dear to my heart;
2. Over the riv-er they call me, Hark, 'tis their voices I hear,
3. Over the riv-er, how love-ly, There is no sorrow nor night;
4. Over the riv-er they call me, Watching with glad, beaming eyes;

Soon shall I meet them in glo- ry, Never, no nev-er to part.
Borne on the wings of the twi-light, Murmuring soft-ly and clear.
There they are walking with Je- sus, Clothed in his garment of light.
O-ver the riv-er I'm com-ing, Joyful my spir-it re-plies.

CHORUS.

O- ver the riv - er to E - den, Home to their dwelling so fair;
An- gels will car - ry me safe - ly, Je- sus will welcome me there.

Copyright, 1892, by Jno. R. Sweney.

Never to Say Farewell.

Rev. Elisha. A. Hoffman. Ira Orwig Hoffman. By per.

Copyright, 1891, by the Hoffman Music Co.

3 We'll meet beyond life's swelling flood,
  Never to say farewell,
Redeemed and washed in Jesus' blood,
  Never to say farewell;
Earth's long, long night will pass away,
Dissolving into heavenly day,
And we shall with our loved ones stay,
  Never to say farewell.

4 Oh, what a blessed hope is this,
  Never to say farewell!
What pure and perfect happiness,
  Never to say farewell!
Delivered from all sin and pain,
To reach yon fair, celestial plain,
And meet the loved and lost again,
  Never to say farewell.

*Very effective if unison parts are sung as a solo.

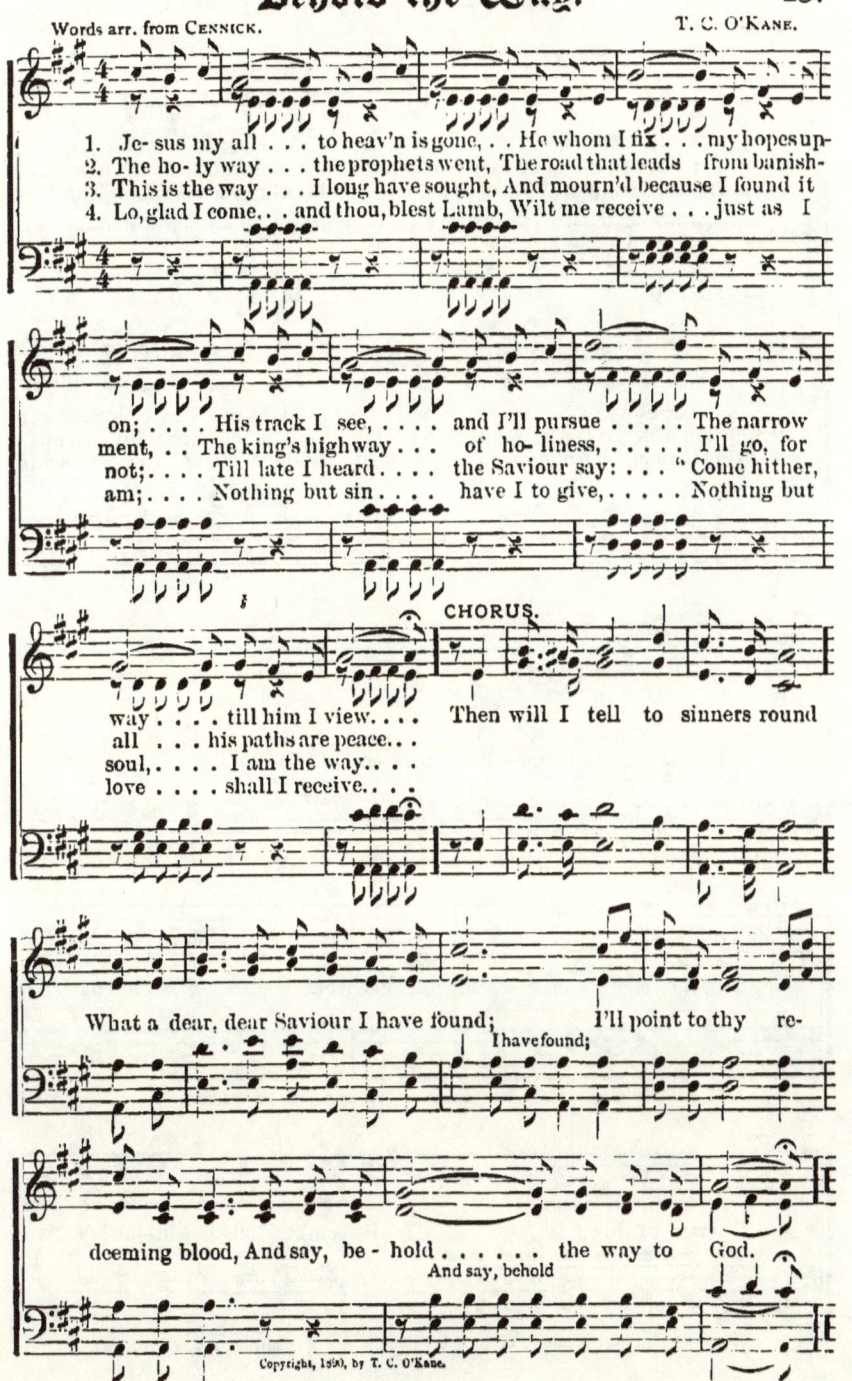

The Coming of His Feet.—CONCLUDED.

...coming robed in light! I lis-ten for the coming of his feet.

4 Sandaled not with shoon of silver,
  girdled not with woven gold,
Weighted not with shimm'ring gems
  and odors sweet,
White-winged and shod with glory in
  the Tabor-light of old—
The glory of the coming of his feet.

5 He is coming, O my spirit! with his
  everlasting peace,
With his blessedness immortal and
  complete;
He is coming, O my spirit! and his
  coming brings release;
I listen for the coming of his feet.

Glory to His Name.

Rev. E. A. Hoffman.   "I will glorify thy name forevermore."   Rev. J. H. Stockton.

1. Down at the cross where my Saviour died, Down where for cleansing from
2. I am so wondrously saved from sin, Je-sus so sweetly a-
3. Oh, precious fountain, that saves from sin! I am so glad I have
4. Come to this fountain, so rich and sweet; Cast thy poor soul at the

sin I cried; There to my heart was the blood ap-plied; Glo-ry to his
bides within; There at the cross where he took me in; Glo-ry to his
entered in; There Jesus saves me and keeps me clean; Glo-ry to his
Saviour's feet; Plunge in to-day, and be made complete; Glo-ry to his

D.S.—There to my heart was the blood applied; Glo-ry to his

Fine. CHORUS.   D.S.

name. Glo-ry to his name, Glo-ry to his name;

By permission.

142. Companionship with Jesus.

MARY D. JAMES.   WM. J. KIRKPATRICK.

1. Oh, bless-ed fel-low-ship divine! Oh, joy supremely sweet! Com-pan-ion-ship with Je-sus here Makes life with bliss re-plete. In un-ion with the pur-est one I find my heav'n on earth be-gun.

2. I'm walking close to Je-sus' side, So close that I can hear The soft-est wisp-ers of his love, In fel-low-ship so dear, And feel his great, al-might-y hand Protects me in this hos-tile land.

3. I'm lean-ing on his lov-ing breast, Along life's weary way; My path, il-lumined by his smiles, Grows brighter day by day. No foes, no woes my heart can fear, With my al-might-y Friend so near.

4. I know his shelt'ring wings of love Are always o'er me spread, And tho' the storms may fiercely rage, All calm and free from dread, My peace-ful spir-it ev-er sings, "I'll trust the cov-ert of thy wings."

CHORUS.

Oh, wondrous bliss! oh, joy sublime! I've Je-sus with me all the time,

Oh, wondrous bliss! oh, joy sublime! I've Je-sus with me all the time.

Copyright, 1876, by WM. J. KIRKPATRICK.

The Song of the Soul. 143

Rev. Henry A. von Dulsem.　　　　　　　　　　　　T. C. O'Kane.

1. Oh, the song of the soul shall not die nor grow old, Nor languish nor pine in the home of our King! But as ages fly onward new chords shall unfold, New melodies meeting inspire us to sing.
2. In the beau-ti-ful land far a-way o'er the tide, The jasper-walled home of the Ancient of Days, Where the ransomed ones shine as the sun in his pride, Our long hal-le-lujahs of glo-ry we'll raise.
3. And the fair, golden harps in the hands of the blest, Shall thrill to a touch that no angel can give, As we sing, in that land where the weary shall rest, Of One who hath died that a sinner might live.
4. And as a-ges fly onward, tho' worlds cease to be, And per-ish the stars that in heaven do throng, Still the joy of the soul shall be deathless and free, And deathless and free the sweet notes of her song.

REFRAIN.

Oh, the song of the soul! Oh, the song of the soul! Forev-er in glo-ry the song of the soul!

Copyright, 1880, by T. C. O'Kane.

The Clear Light, etc.—CONCLUDED. 145

me he's far dear-er Than all else be-side.

Do the Right.

NORMAN MACLEOD, D. D.   PHILIP PHILLIPS.

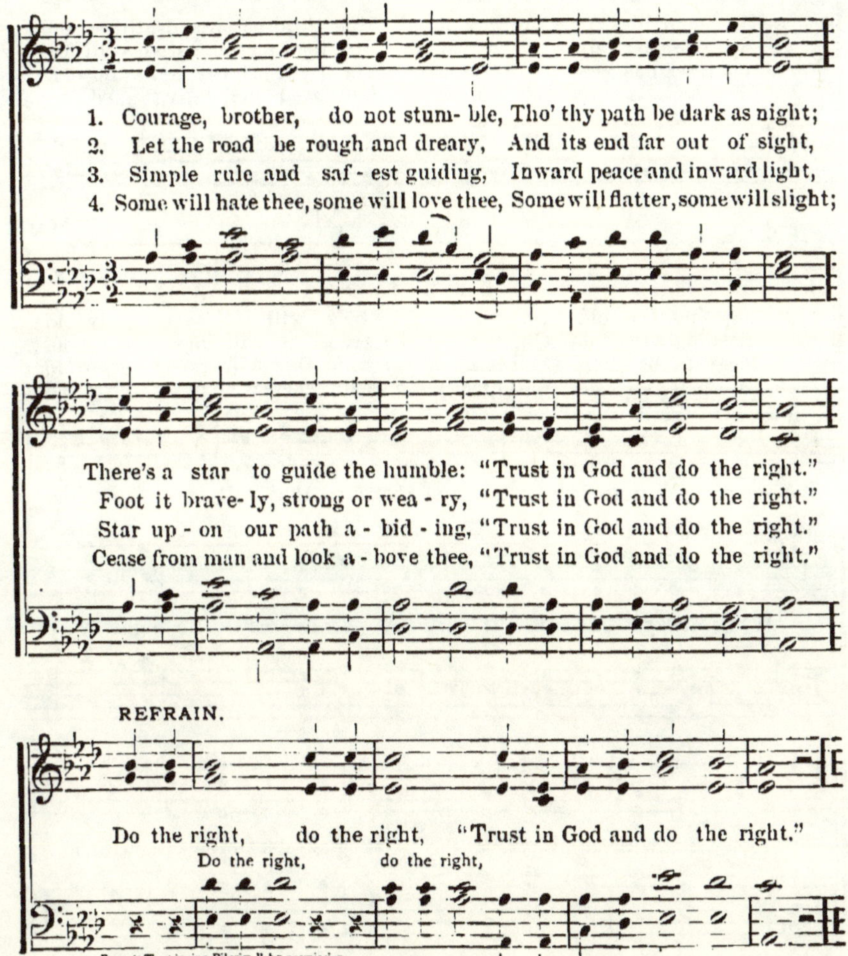

1. Courage, brother, do not stum-ble, Tho' thy path be dark as night;
2. Let the road be rough and dreary, And its end far out of sight,
3. Simple rule and saf-est guiding, Inward peace and inward light,
4. Some will hate thee, some will love thee, Some will flatter, some will slight;

There's a star to guide the humble: "Trust in God and do the right."
Foot it brave-ly, strong or wea-ry, "Trust in God and do the right."
Star up-on our path a-bid-ing, "Trust in God and do the right."
Cease from man and look a-bove thee, "Trust in God and do the right."

REFRAIN.

Do the right, do the right, "Trust in God and do the right."
Do the right, do the right,

From "The Singing Pilgrim," by permission.

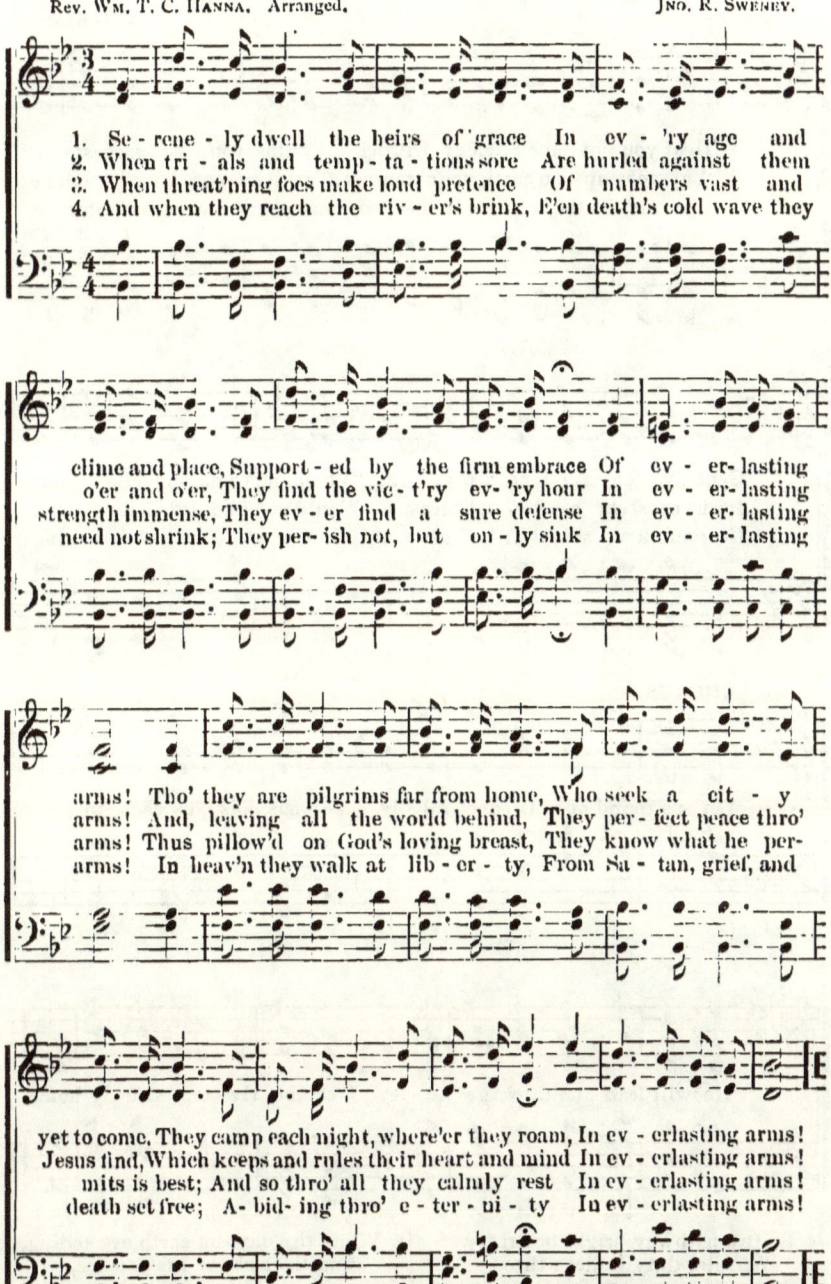

Follow Me.

T. C. O'K. T. C. O'Kane.

1. Hear you not the Saviour calling, Calling you so earnest-ly?
2. Lay not up on earth your treasure, Transient, perish-ing 'twill be;
3. In my Father's house in heaven, Let your hearts untroubled be,

Gent-ly, too, the tones are fall-ing, "Come, oh, come, and follow me."
Rath-er seek e-ter-nal pleasure; Would you find it? follow me.
Glorious man-sion will be giv-en, On-ly come and follow me.

CHORUS.

Let us round our Leader ral-ly, Je-sus bids us each to come;

He will lead us thro' the val-ley, O'er the riv-er, safe-ly home.

4 Be thy pathway bright or dreary
   Whither duty leadeth thee,
   Strong thy steps, or faint and weary,
   I will guide thee,—follow me.

5 When thy days on earth are ending,
   And the close of life you see,
   Even to the grave descending,
   Never fear, but follow me.

By permission.

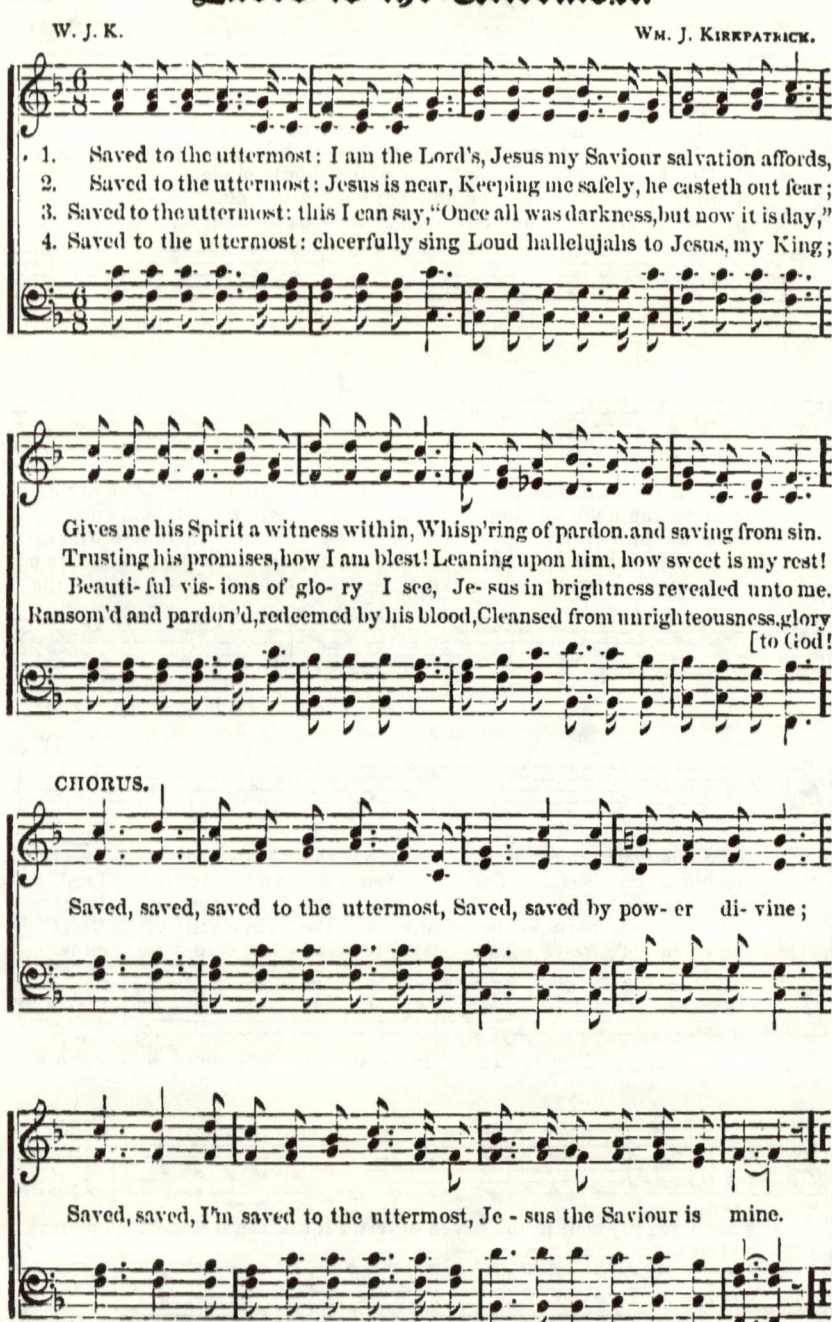

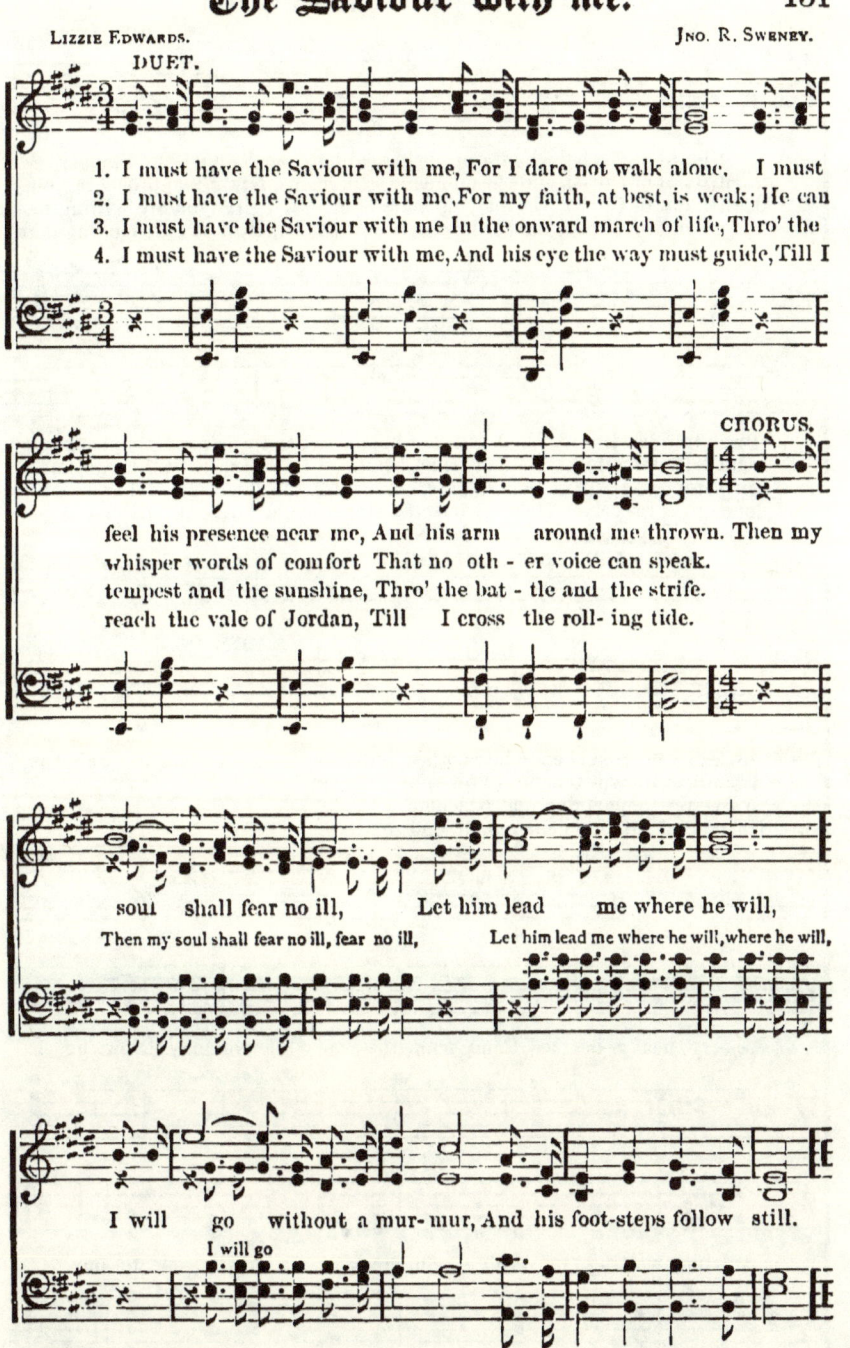

152. Still out of Christ.

H. E. BLAIR.
WM. J. KIRKPATRICK.

1. Still out of Christ, when so oft he has called you, Why will you longer refuse to believe? What can you hope from the world or its pleasure? How can you trust them when both will deceive?
2. Still out of Christ, and the moments so precious, Night is approaching, oh, what will you do? Still out of Christ, yet there's room at the fountain, Free are its waters, and flowing for you.
3. Still out of Christ, yet for you there is mercy, If you are willing to turn from your sin; Yonder he stands at the door of salvation, Waiting to pardon and welcome you in.
4 Still out of Christ, and the love he has promised, How you are longing that love to receive: Haste where the star of your faith is directing, Haste, and this moment repent and believe.

REFRAIN.

Come, come to Jesus, weary, heavy-hearted, Come, come to Jesus while you may; Now he is waiting, waiting to receive you, Hark, he is calling you to-day.

Copyright, 1886, by Wm. J. Kirkpatrick.

Why Still Unsaved To-night? 153

Elisha Hoffman.   T. C. O'Kane.

1. The ten-der voice of Je-sus has oft-en thrill'd thy heart,
2. The Lord has lavished bless-ings pro-fuse-ly on thy way,
3. Come, give thyself to Je-sus, who died to ran-som thee,

Be-seeching thee in gen-tle tones from all thy sins to part;
Ten thousand are the mer-cies rich he sends thee day by day;
Come, bring thy heart so press'd with sin, and he will set it free;

Why do you all the call-ings of the blessed Spir-it slight?
Why with in-grat-i-tude do you the love of God requite?
O do not now a-gain the call of thy Re-deem-er slight,

ritard.

O soul, for whom the Saviour died, why still unsaved to-night?
O soul, for whom the Saviour died, why still unsaved to-night?
Per-haps thy la-test call may be the call that comes to-night.

D.S.—O soul, for whom the Saviour died, why still unsaved to-night?

REFRAIN. *Slow'y.*   D.S.

1st & 2d.—Why still unsaved to-night? Why still unsaved to-night?
3d.—Why not be saved to-night? Why not be saved to-night?

From "Happy Songs."

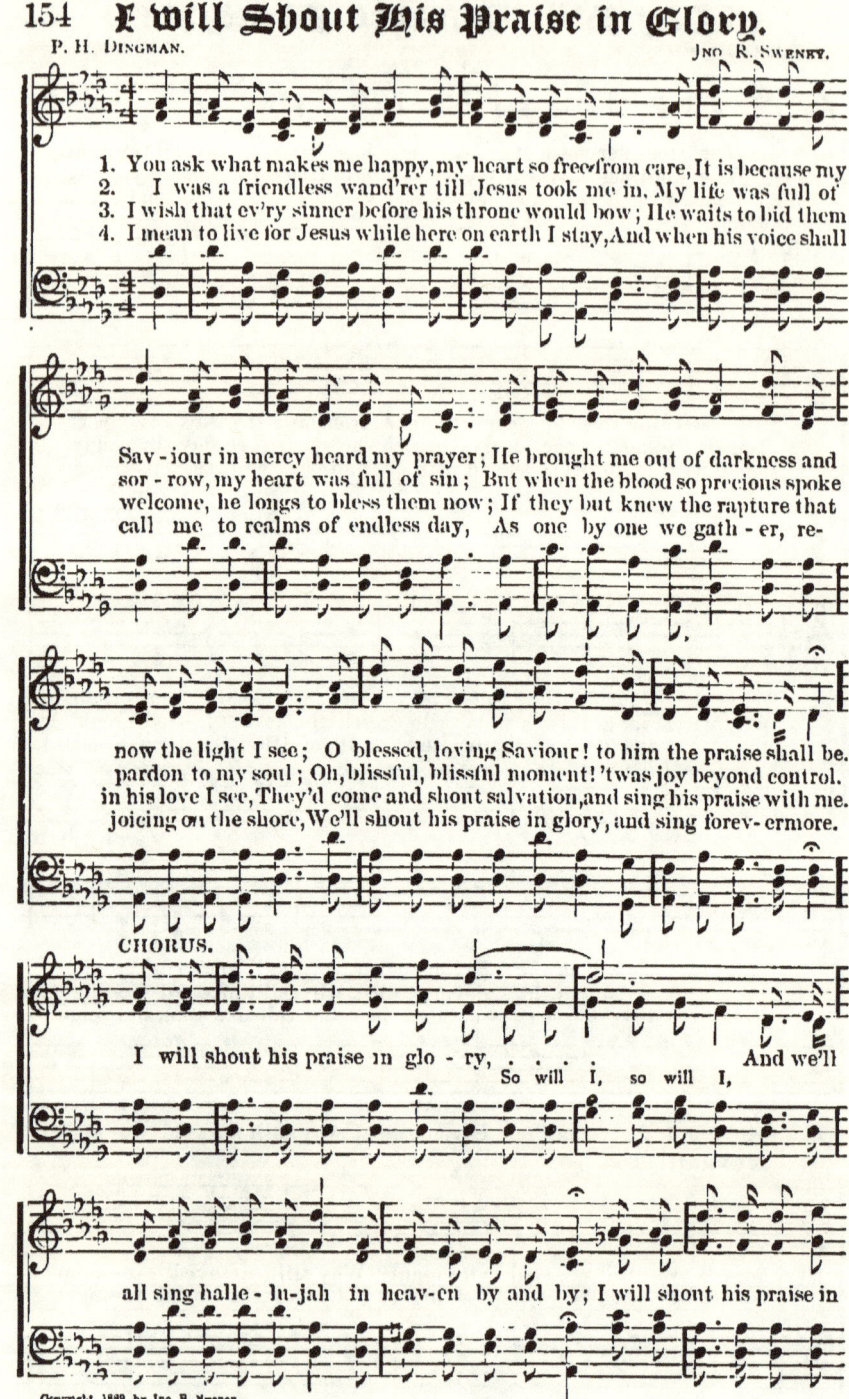

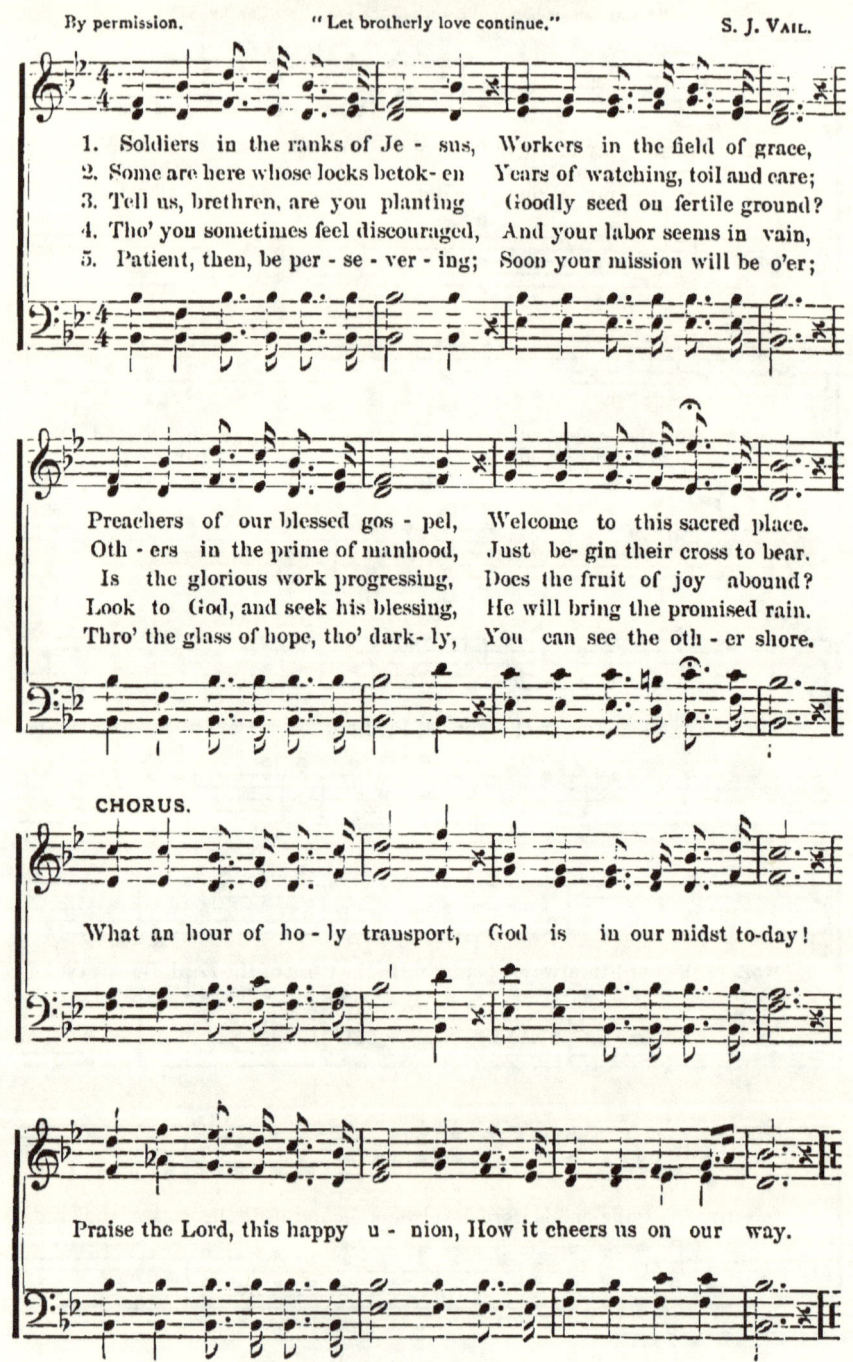

Though Your Sins be as Scarlet. 161

"Though your sins be as scarlet, they shall be as white as snow."—Isaiah i. 18.

FANNY J. CROSBY.   W. H. DOANE. By per.

DUET. *Gently.* |1st. |2nd.

1. "Tho' your sins be as scarlet, They shall be as white as snow; as snow:
2.   Hear the voice that entreats you, Oh, return ye unto God! to God!
3. He'll forgive your transgressions, And remember them no more; no more;

QUARTET.

Tho' they be red . . . . like crimson, They shall be as wool;"
He is of great . . . compassion, And of wondrous love;
"Look un-to me, . . . ye people," Saith the Lord your God;

Tho' they be red

DUET. *p*   QUARTET. *f*

"Tho' your sins be as scarlet, Tho' your sins be as scarlet,
Hear the voice that entreats you, Hear the voice that entreats you,
He'll forgive your transgressions, He'll forgive your transgressions,

p ritard.

They shall be as white as snow, They shall be as white as snow."
Oh, return ye un-to God! Oh, return ye un-to God!
And remem - ber them no more, And remem - ber them no more.

Copyright, 1887, by W. H. Doane.

Unfading Treasures—L   11

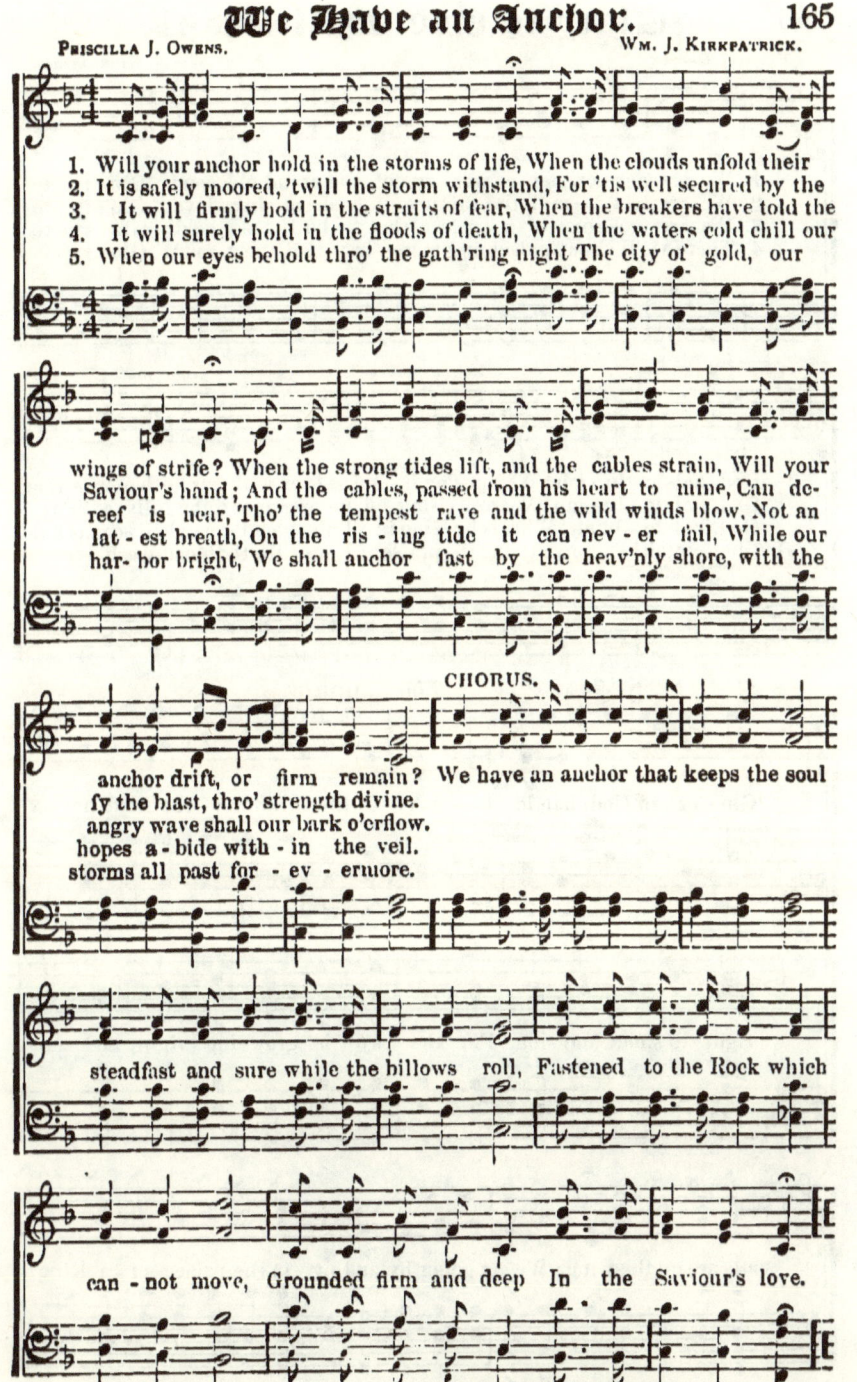

168 Leaning on Jesus.

Rev. W. F. Crafts.   Wm. J. Kirkpatrick.

1. Wea-ry with walking a-lone, Long heav-y-laden with sin;
2. Fearing to stand for my Lord, Trembling for weakness in prayer;

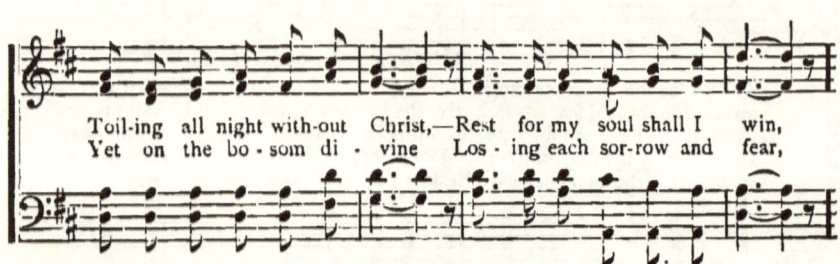

Toil-ing all night with-out Christ,—Rest for my soul shall I win,
Yet on the bo-som di-vine Los-ing each sor-row and fear,

CHORUS.

Lean - ing on Je - sus, I walk at his side;
Leaning on Je-sus, in him I a-bide. Leaning on Je-sus, I walk at his side;

Lean - - ing on Je - - sus, I trust him, my Shepherd and Guide.
Leaning on Je-sus, what-ev-er be-tide,

3 Anxious no longer for self,
   Shrinking no longer from pain,
  Leaning on Jesus alone,
   He all my care will sustain.

4 Leaning, I walk in "the way,"
   Leaning, "the truth" I shall know;
  Leaning on heart-throbs of Christ,
   Safe into "life" I may go.

From "Leaflet Gems," by permission of John J. Hood.

Leaning on the Everlasting Arms. 171

Rev. E. A. Hoffman.   A. J. Showalter.

1. What a fel-lowship, what a joy divine, Leaning on the ev-er-
2. Oh, how sweet to walk in this pilgrim way, Leaning on the ev-er-
3. What have I to dread, what have I to fear, Leaning on the ev-er-

last-ing arms; What a bless-ed-ness, What a peace is mine,
last-ing arms; Oh, how bright the path grows from day to day,
last-ing arms? I have bless-ed peace with my Lord so near,

REFRAIN.

Lean-ing on the ev-er-last-ing arms. Lean - ing,
Lean-ing on the ev-er-last-ing arms.
Lean-ing on the ev-er-last-ing arms. Lean-ing on Je-sus,

lean - ing, Safe and se-cure from all a-larms;
Lean-ing on Je-sus,

Lean - ing, lean - ing, Leaning on the ev-er-lasting arms.
Lean-ing on Je-sus, lean-ing on Je-sus,

By per. A. J. Showalter.

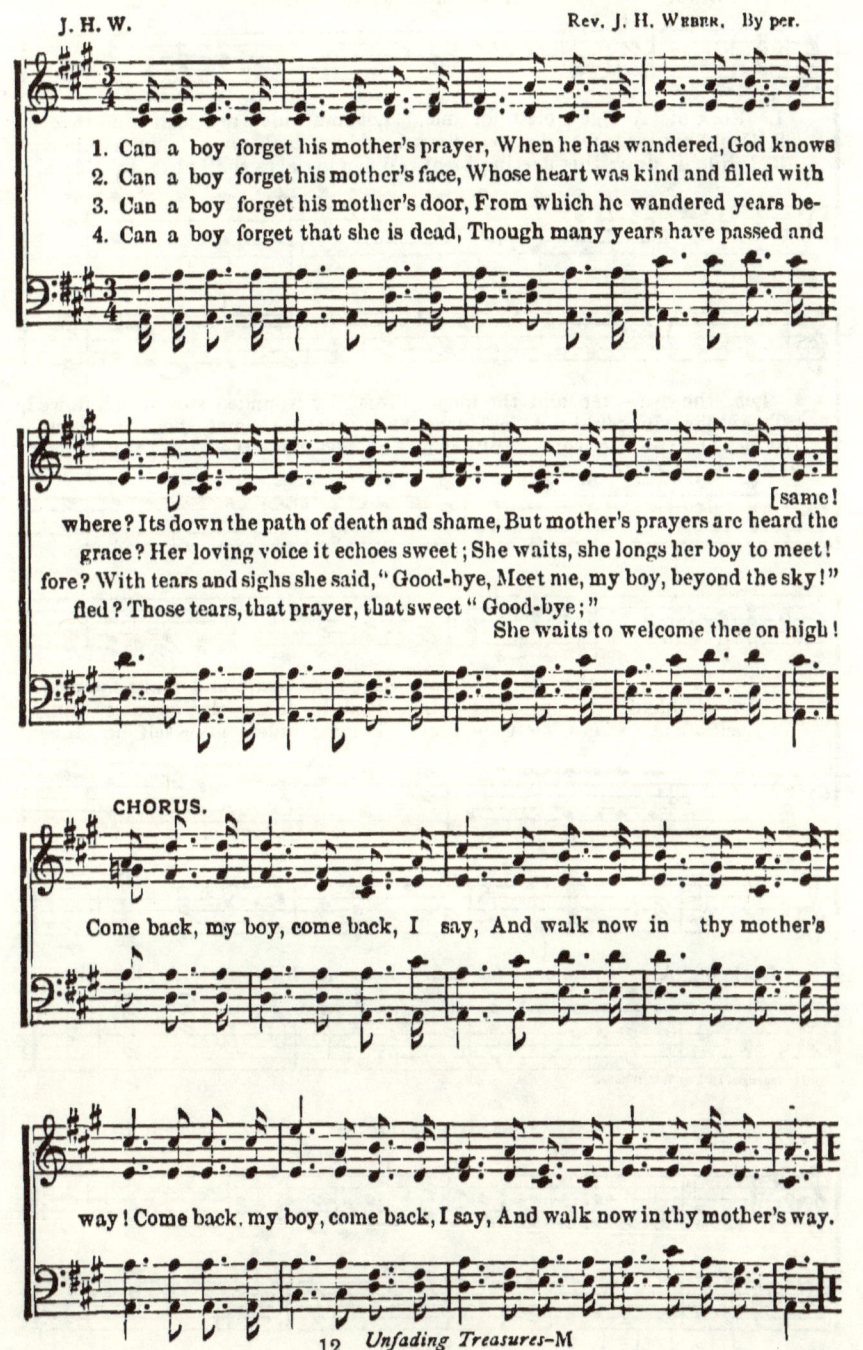

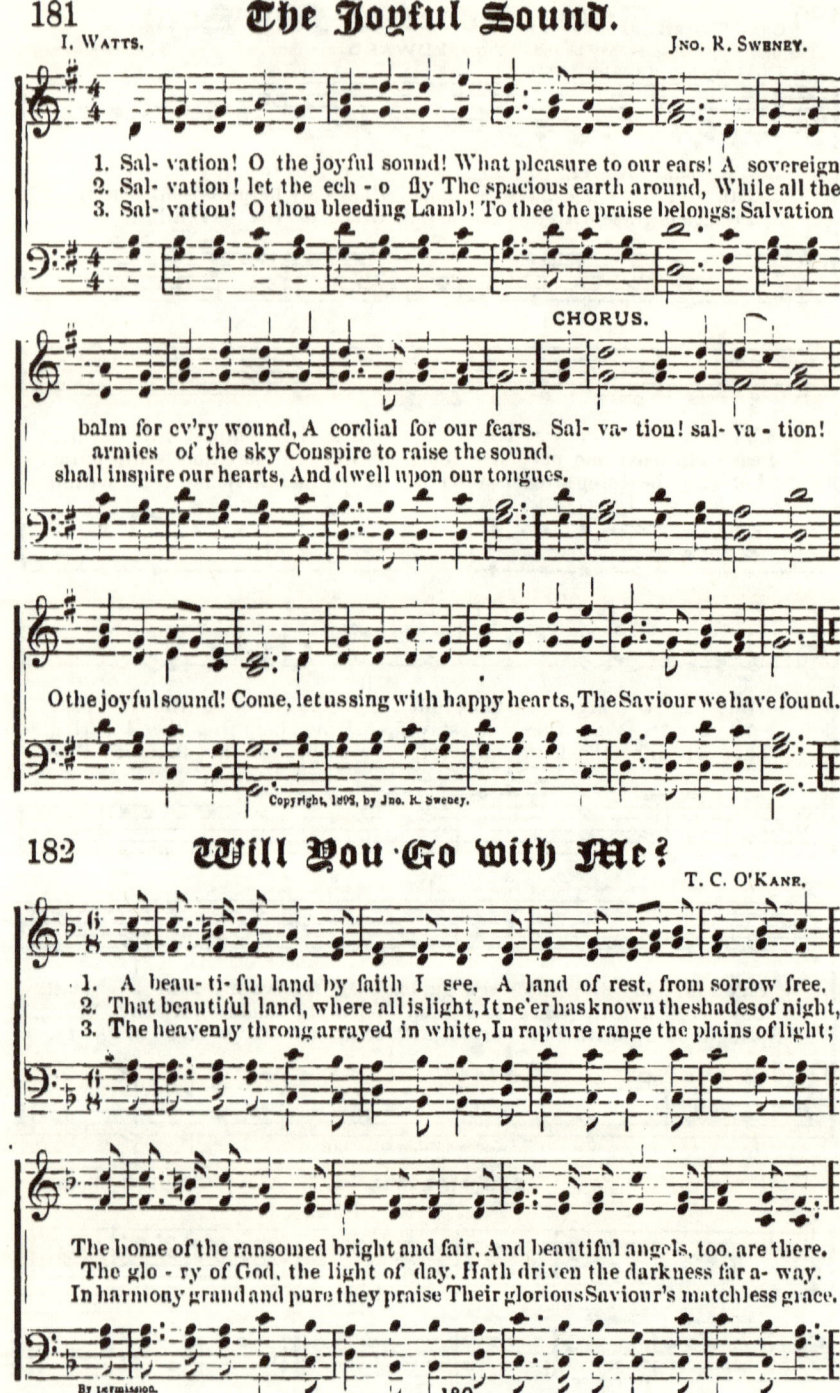

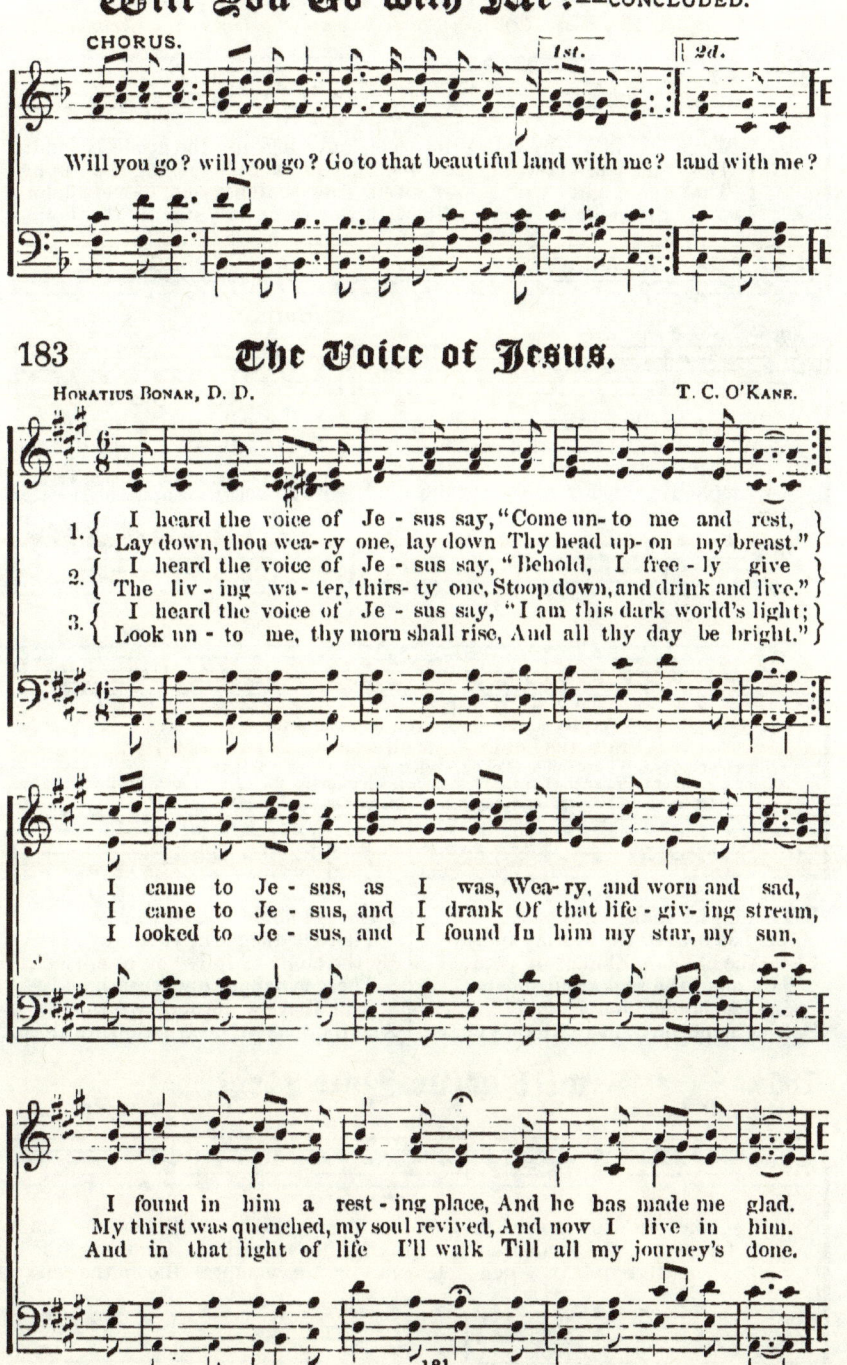

184. We are Sailing O'er the Sea.

I. B.   "They came over to the other side of the sea."—Mark v: 1.   I. Baltzell.

1. We're a happy, pilgrim band, Sailing to the goodly land;
Tho' the tempest rages long, There is One among the throng

2. Tho' the mighty billows swell, They shall never o-verwhelm,
'Mid the strife his praise will swell, For we've Jesus at the helm,

Chorus.
With a swelling sail we onward sweep;
Who will guide the sailor o'er the deep.
Tho' the breakers roll up-on the lea;
And he'll guide her safely o'er the sea.

We are sailing o'er the sea, We are sailing o'er the sea;
We are sailing, sailing, sailing, we are sailing o'er the sea;
Praise the Lord, we'll soon be free, yes, praise the Lord, we'll soon be free.

By permission.

3 Though for many ages past
She has braved the stormy blast,
She's the old ship Zion as of yore;
Safe amid the rocks and shoals
She has landed many souls,
Safe at home, on Canaan's happy shore.

4 Ho! ye sinners, hear to-day,
There is danger in your way!
By the chart of folly you're misled;
There is danger underneath,
And above a storm of wrath,
And the rocks of destruction are ahead

185. I Will Give You Rest.

Mrs. C. H. Esling.   T. C. O'Kane.

1. Come un-to me when shadows darkly gather, When the sad
2. Large are the mansions in thy Father's dwelling, Glad are the
3. There, like an Eden blossoming in gladness, Bloom the fair

187. Gathering One by One.

T. C. O'K. T. C. O'Kane.

1. "One by one," the bonds are severed, Binding hearts together here;
   "One by one," new ties are add-ed To the land that
2. "One by one" we cease our toil-ing For the Mas-ter here be-low;
   By the an-gel bands attend-ed, To our end-less

CHORUS.

knows no tear. Gath'ring home, gath'ring home, "One by one," we're gathering
rest we go.

Repeat chorus pp.

home; Soon we'll all be gathered home, Gathered "one by one."

From "Songs of Worship."

3 "One by one," we're gath'ring yon-
   Out of every clime and land; [der,
   "One by one" we're crossing over,
   To the distant heavenly strand.

4 "One by one" the Saviour calls us
   In his perfect bliss to share;
   May we for the call be ready—
   Oh, may none be missing there!

188. Come, Holy Spirit.

I. Watts. Jno. R. Sweney.

1. Come, Ho-ly Spir-it, heavenly Dove, With all thy quick'ning powers;
2. Look how we grov-el here be-low, Fond of these earth-ly toys;
3. In vain we tune our for-mal songs, In vain we strive to rise;
4. Father, and shall we ev-er live At this poor dy-ing rate,
5. Come, Ho-ly Spir-it, heavenly Dove, With all thy quick'ning powers;

Copyright, 1883, by John R. Sweney.

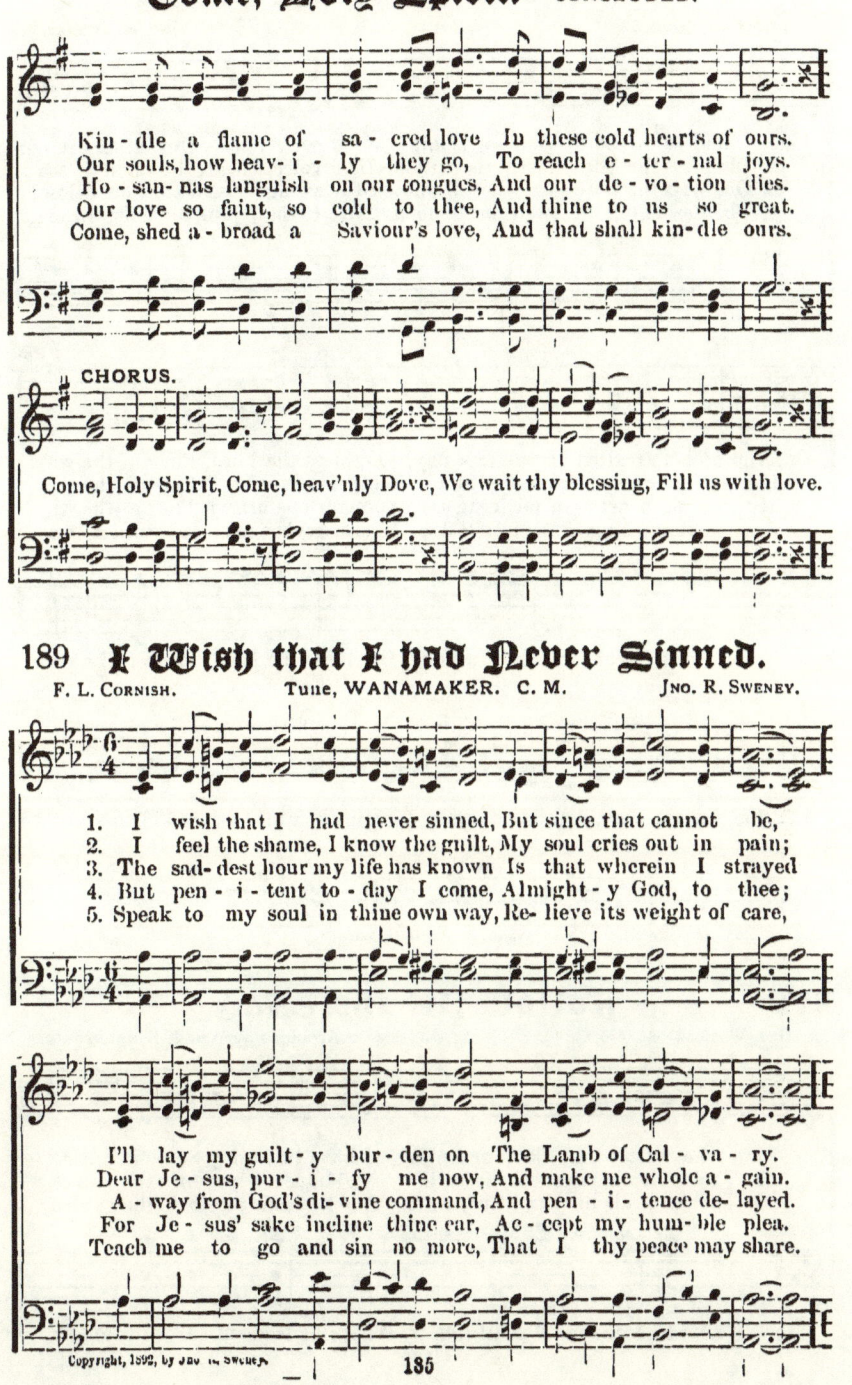

Follow All the Way.—CONCLUDED.

I have heard my Saviour calling, "Take thy cross and follow, follow me."
Tho' he leads me thro' the valley, I'll go with him, with him all the way.
Tho' he leads me thro' the garden, I'll go with him, with him all the way.

Where he leads me I will follow, I'll go with him, with him all the way.

4 ‖: Tho' the path be dark and dreary, :‖
I'll go with him, with him all the way.

5 ‖: Tho' he leads me to the conflict, :‖
I'll go with him, with him all the way.

6 ‖: Tho' he leads through fiery trials, :‖
I'll go with him, with him all the way.

7 ‖: I will follow on to know him, :‖
He's my Saviour, Saviour, Brother, Friend.

8 ‖: He will give me grace and glory, :‖
He will keep me, keep me all the way.

9 ‖: O 'tis sweet to follow Jesus, :‖
And be with him, with him all the way.

192 The Golden Key.

"Prayer is the key to unlock the door, and the bolt to shut in the night."

JNO. R. SWENEY.

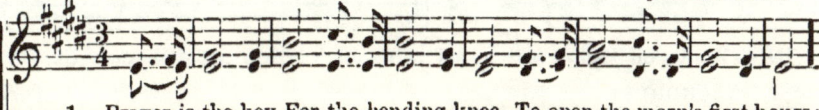

1. Prayer is the key For the bending knee To open the morn's first hours;
2. Not a soul so sad, Nor a heart so glad, When cometh the shades of night,
3. Take the golden key In your hand and see, As the night tide drifts away,

See the incense rise To the starry skies, Like perfume from the flow'rs.
But the daybreak song Will the joy prolong, And some darkness turn to light.
How its blessed hold Is a crown of gold, Thro' the weary hours of day.

Copyright, 1875, by John J. Hood.

4 When the shadows fall,
And the vesper call
Is sobbing its low refrain,
'Tis a garland sweet
To the toil-dent feet,
And an antidote for pain.

5 Soon the year's dark door
Shall be shut no more:
Life's tears shall be wiped away,
As the pearl gates swing,
And the gold harps ring,
And the sun unsheathes for aye.

Sometimes a Light, etc.—CONCLUDED.

When comforts are de-clin-ing, He grants the soul a-gain

2 In holy contemplation,
    We sweetly then pursue
  The theme of God's salvation,
    And find it ever new:
  Set free from present sorrow,
    We cheerfully can say,
  Let the unknown to-morrow
    Bring with it what it may.

3 It can bring with it nothing
    But he will bear us through;
  Who gives the lilies clothing,
    Will clothe his people too:
  Beneath the spreading heavens
    No creature but is fed;
  And he who feeds the ravens
    Will give his children bread.

195   I Do Believe.

CHAS. WESLEY. — C. M.

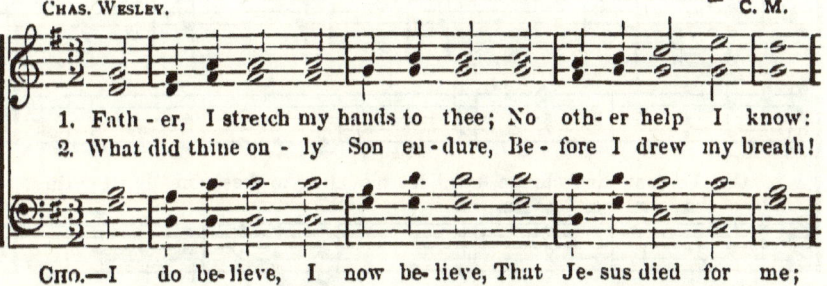

1. Fath-er, I stretch my hands to thee; No oth-er help I know:
2. What did thine on-ly Son en-dure, Be-fore I drew my breath!

CHO.—I do be-lieve, I now be-lieve, That Je-sus died for me;

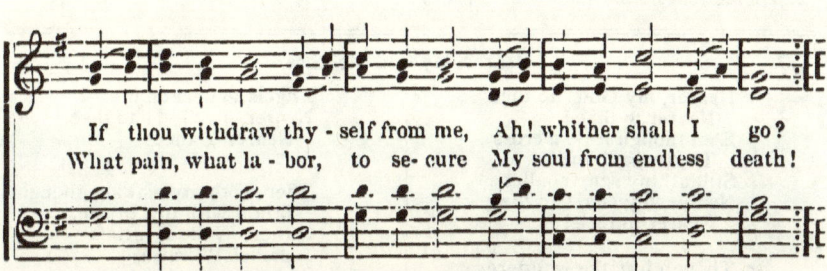

If thou withdraw thy-self from me, Ah! whither shall I go?
What pain, what la-bor, to se-cure My soul from endless death!

And thro' his blood, his precious blood, I shall from sin be free.

3 O Jesus, could I this believe,
    I now should feel thy power;
  And all my wants thou wouldst relieve,
    In this accepted hour.

4 Author of faith! to thee I lift
    My weary, longing eyes:
  Oh, let me now receive that gift;
    My soul without it dies.

5 Surely thou canst not let me die;
    Oh, speak, and I shall live;
  And here I will unwearied lie,
    Till thou thy Spirit give.

6 How would my fainting soul rejoice
    Could I but see thy face!
  Now let me hear thy quickening voice,
    And taste thy pardoning grace.

197. Nearer, My God! to Thee.

1 Nearer, my God! to thee,
 Nearer to thee!
E'en though it be a cross
 That raiseth me!
Still all my song shall be,
Nearer, my God! to thee,
 Nearer to thee!

2 Though like the wanderer,
 The sun gone down,
Darkness be over me,
 My rest a stone,
Yet in my dreams I'd be
Nearer, my God! to thee,
 Nearer to thee!

3 There let the way appear,
 Steps unto heaven;
All that thou sendest me,
 In mercy given;

Angels to beckon me
Nearer, my God! to thee,
 Nearer to thee!

4 Then, with my waking thoughts
 Bright with thy praise,
Out of my stony griefs
 Bethel I'll raise;
So by my woes to be
Nearer, my God! to thee,
 Nearer to thee!

5 Or if, on joyful wing
 Cleaving the sky,
Sun, moon and stars forgot,
 Upward I fly,
Still all my song shall be,
Nearer, my God! to thee,
 Nearer to thee!

198. Revive us again.

Wm. P. Mackay.   J. J. Husband

1. We praise thee, O God! for the Son of thy love,
For Jesus who died and is now gone above.

REFRAIN.
Hal-le-lujah! thine the glory; Halle-lujah! a-men! Revive us a-gain.

2 We praise thee, O God! for thy Spirit of light,
Who has shown us our Saviour and scattered our night.
3 All glory and praise to the Lamb that was slain,
Who has borne all our sins, and has cleansed every stain.
4 All glory and praise to the God of all grace,
Who has bought us, and sought us, and guided our ways.

199. Faithful Guide.

M. M. Wells. By per.

1. Ho-ly Spir-it, faith-ful guide, Ev-er near the Christian's side;
Gen-tly lead us by the hand, Pil-grims in a des-ert land;
D.C. Whisp'ring soft-ly, wan-d'rer, come! Follow me, I'll guide thee home.

Wea-ry souls for e'er re-joice, While they hear that sweet-est voice,

2 Ever present, truest Friend,
Ever near thine aid to lend,
Leave us not to doubt and fear,
Groping on in darkness drear,
When the storms are raging sore,
Hearts grow faint, and hopes give o'er,
Whispering softly, wanderer, come!
Follow me, I'll guide thee home.

3 When our days of toil shall cease,
Waiting still for sweet release,
Nothing left but heaven and prayer,
Wond'ring if our names were there;
Wading deep the dismal flood,
Pleading nought but Jesus' blood;
Whispering softly, wanderer, come!
Follow me, I'll guide thee home!

200. The Gospel Feast.

CHARLES WESLEY.
Cho. by H. L. G.
"Come, for all things are ready"
Luke xiv: 16.
H. L. GILMOUR. By per.

1. Come, sinners, to the gos-pel feast; It is for you, it is for me;
2. Ye need not one be left behind, It is for you, it is for me;

Let ev-'ry soul be Je-sus' guest; It is for you, it is for me.
For God hath bidden all mankind, It is for you, it is for me.

D.S.—O wea-ry wand'rer, come and see, It is for you, it is for me.

CHORUS. D.S.

Sal-vation full, sal-vation free, The price was paid on Cal-va-ry;

Copyright, 1889, by H. L. Gilmour.

3 Sent by my Lord, on you I call;
  The invitation is to all:
4 Come, all the world! come, sinner thou!
  All things in Christ are ready now.
5 Come, all ye souls by sin oppressed,
  Ye restless wanderers after rest:
6 Ye poor, and maimed, and halt, and blind
  In Christ a hearty welcome find.

7 My message as from God receive;
  Ye all may come to Christ and live:
8 O let this love your hearts constrain,
  Nor suffer him to die in vain.
9 See him set forth before your eyes,
  That precious, bleeding sacrifice:
10 His offered benefits embrace,
   And freely now be saved by grace.

201. Loving Kindness.

MEDLEY.

1. Awake, my soul to joyful lays, And sing thy great Redeemer's praise;
2. He saw me ru-ined in the fall, Yet loved me not-withstanding all;

Loving Kindness.—CONCLUDED.

He just-ly claims a song from me, His lov-ing-kind-ness, oh, how free!
He saved me from my lost e-state, His lov-ing-kind-ness, oh, how great!

Lov-ing-kindness, lov-ing-kindness, His lov-ing-kind-ness, oh, how free!
Lov-ing-kindness, lov-ing-kindness, His lov-ing-kind-ness, oh, how great!

3 Though num'rous hosts of mighty foes,
Though earth and hell my way oppose,
He safely leads my soul along,
His loving-kindness, oh, how strong!

4 When trouble, like a gloomy cloud,
Has gathered thick, and thundered loud,
He near my soul has always stood,
His loving-kindness, oh, how good!

202. My Faith Looks Up to Thee.

Ray Palmer.   L. Mason.

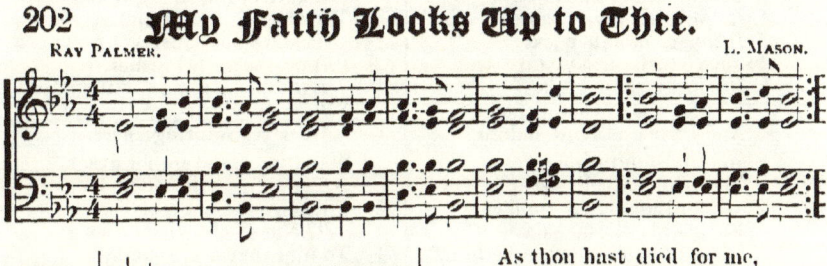

1 My faith looks up to thee,
Thou Lamb of Calvary,
  Saviour divine!
Now hear me while I pray;
Take all my guilt away;
Oh, let me from this day
  Be wholly thine!

2 May thy rich grace impart
Strength to my fainting heart,
  My zeal inspire!

As thou hast died for me,
Oh, may my love to thee
Pure, warm, and changeless be—
  A living fire!

3 While life's dark maze I tread,
And griefs around me spread,
  Be thou my guide;
Bid darkness turn to day,
Wipe sorrow's tears away,
Nor let me ever stray
  From thee aside.

4 When ends life's transient dream,
When death's cold sullen stream
  Shall o'er me roll,
Blest Saviour! then, in love,
Fear and distrust remove;
Oh, bear me safe above—
  A ransomed soul!

203. The Morning Light.

SAMUEL F. SMITH. Tune, WEBB. 7, 6.

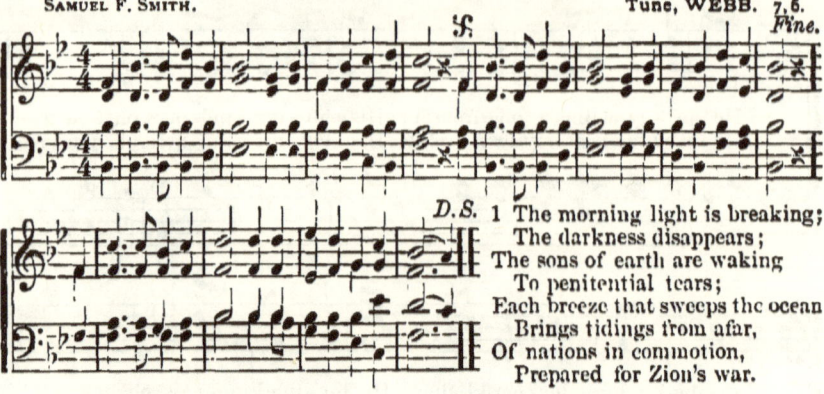

1 The morning light is breaking;
 The darkness disappears;
 The sons of earth are waking
 To penitential tears;
 Each breeze that sweeps the ocean
 Brings tidings from afar,
 Of nations in commotion,
 Prepared for Zion's war.

2 See heathen nations bending
 Before the God we love,
 And thousand hearts ascending
 In gratitude above;
 While sinners, now confessing,
 The gospel call obey,
 And seek the Saviour's blessing,
 A nation in a day.

3 Blest river of salvation,
 Pursue thine onward way;
 Flow thou to every nation,
 Nor in thy richness stay;
 Stay not till all the lowly
 Triumphant reach their home;
 Stay not till all the holy
 Proclaim, "The Lord is come!"

204. Stand up, stand up for Jesus.

GEO. DUFFIELD, Jr. Tune above.

1 STAND up, stand up for Jesus,
 Ye soldiers of the cross;
 Lift high his royal banner,
 It must not suffer loss;
 From victory unto victory
 His army shall he lead
 Till every foe is vanquished
 And Christ is Lord indeed.

2 Stand up, stand up for Jesus,
 The trumpet call obey;
 Forth to the mighty conflict,
 In this his glorious day:
 "Ye that are men, now serve him,"
 Against unnumbered foes;
 Your courage rise with danger,
 And strength to strength oppose.

3 Stand up, stand up for Jesus,
 Stand in his strength alone;
 The arm of flesh will fail you;
 Ye dare not trust your own:
 Put on the gospel armor,
 Each piece put on with prayer;
 Where duty calls, or danger,
 Be never wanting there.

4 Stand up, stand up for Jesus,
 The strife will not be long;
 This day the noise of battle,
 The next the victor's song;
 To him that overcometh,
 A crown of life shall be;
 He with the King of glory
 Shall reign eternally.

205. Work, for the Night is Coming.

1 WORK, for the night is coming,
 Work through the morning hours;
 Work, while the dew is sparkling,
 Work 'mid springing flowers;
 Work, when the days grow brighter,
 Work in the glowing sun;
 Work, for the night is coming,
 When man's work is done.

2 Work, for the night is coming,
 Work through the sunny noon;
 Fill brightest hours with labor,
 Rest comes sure and soon,
 Give every flying minute
 Something to keep in store;
 Work, for the night is coming,
 When man works no more.

3 Work, for the night is coming,
 Under the sunset skies;
 While their bright tints are glowing,
 Work, for daylight flies.
 Work till the last beam fadeth,
 Fadeth to shine no more;
 Work while the night is darkening,
 When man's work is o'er.

206. Come, Ye Disconsolate.

THOMAS MOORE, alt., and THOS. HASTINGS.   SAMUEL WEBBE.

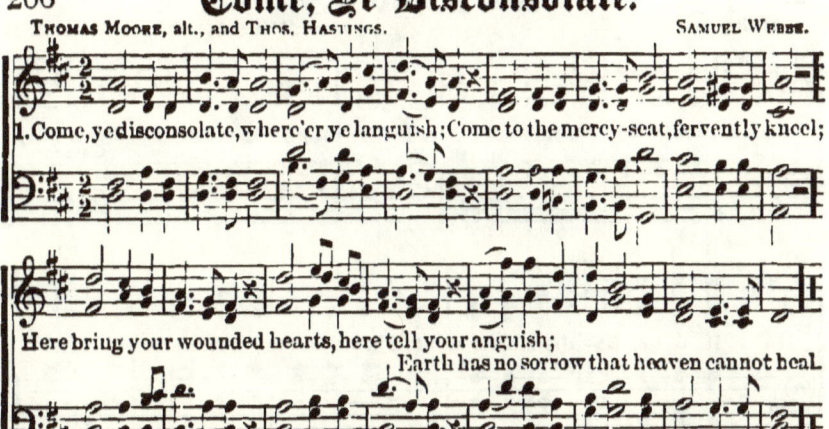

1. Come, ye disconsolate, where'er ye languish; Come to the mercy-seat, fervently kneel; Here bring your wounded hearts, here tell your anguish; Earth has no sorrow that heaven cannot heal.

2 Joy of the desolate, light of the straying,
Hope of the penitent, fadeless and pure,
Here speaks the Comforter, tenderly saying,
"Earth has no sorrow that heaven cannot cure."

3 Here see the bread of life; see waters flowing
Forth from the throne of God, pure from above;
Come to the feast of love; come, ever knowing
Earth has no sorrow but heaven can remove.

207. Rest in Jesus.

W. H. DOANE.

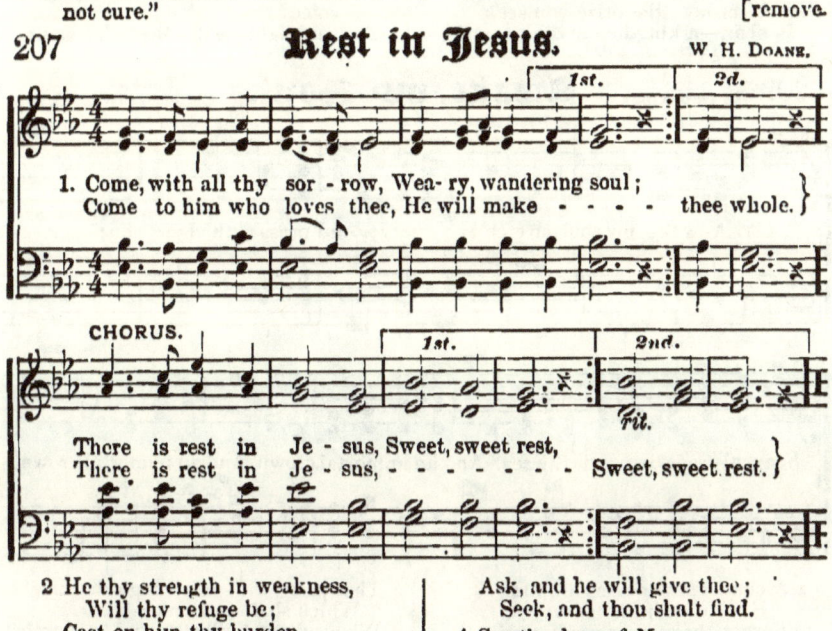

1. Come, with all thy sorrow, Weary, wandering soul;
Come to him who loves thee, He will make thee whole.

CHORUS.
There is rest in Jesus, Sweet, sweet rest,
There is rest in Jesus, Sweet, sweet rest.

2 He thy strength in weakness,
Will thy refuge be;
Cast on him thy burden,
He will care for thee.

3 Come, in faith believing,
To his will resigned;

Ask, and he will give thee;
Seek, and thou shalt find.

4 See the door of Mercy,
Wouldst thou enter there?
Knock, and he will open;
Lo! the key is prayer.

Used by per. of W. H. Doane, owner of Copyright.

208. Go, Labor On.

H. Bonar. Tune, MISSIONARY CHANT. L. M.

1. Go, labor on; spend and be spent, Thy joy to do the Father's will; It is the way the Master went; Should not the servant tread it still?

2 Go, labor on; 'tis not for naught;
   Thine earthly loss is heavenly gain;
   Men heed thee, love thee, praise thee not;
   The Master praises,—what are men?

3 Go, labor on; your hands are weak;
   Your knees are faint, your soul cast down;
   Yet falter not; the prize you seek
   Is near,—a kingdom and a crown!

4 Toil on, faint not; keep watch, and pray!
   Be wise the erring soul to win;
   Go forth into the world's highway;
   Compel the wanderer to come in.

5 Toil on, and in thy toil rejoice;
   For toil comes rest, for exile home;
   Soon shalt thou hear the Bridegroom's voice,
   The midnight peal, "Behold, I come!"

209. Awake, my Soul.

P. Doddridge. Tune, CHRISTMAS. C. M.

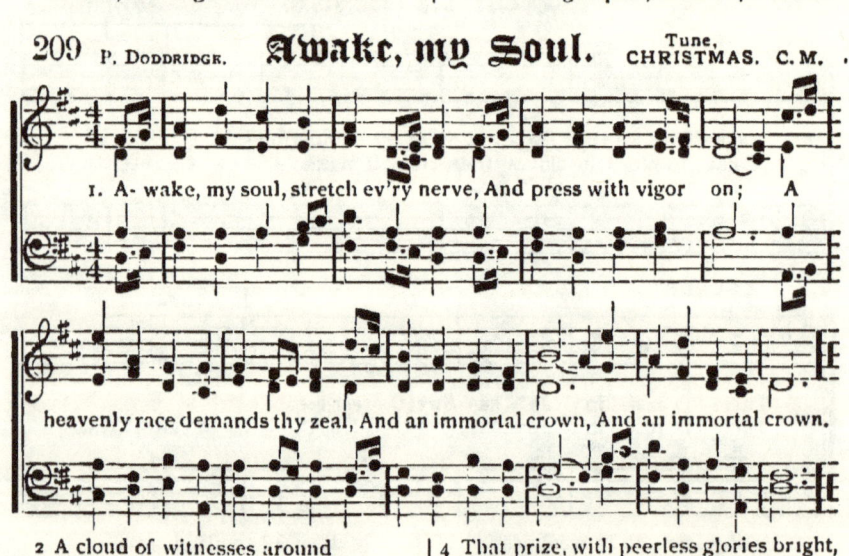

1. A-wake, my soul, stretch ev'ry nerve, And press with vigor on; A heavenly race demands thy zeal, And an immortal crown, And an immortal crown.

2 A cloud of witnesses around
   Hold thee in full survey;
   Forget the steps already trod,
   And onward urge thy way.

3 'Tis God's all-animating voice
   That calls thee from on high;
   'Tis his own hand presents the prize
   To thine aspiring eye:—

4 That prize, with peerless glories bright,
   Which shall new luster boast,
   When victors' wreaths and monarchs' gems
   Shall blend in common dust.

5 Blest Saviour, introduced by thee,
   Have I my race begun;
   And, crowned with victory, at thy feet
   I'll lay my honors down.

Dennis. S. M.

210 Blest be the Tie that Binds.

1 Blest be the tie that binds
  Our hearts in Christian love;
The fellowship of kindred minds
  Is like to that above.

2 Before our Father's throne
  We pour our ardent prayers;
Our fears, our hopes, our aims are one,
  Our comforts and our cares.

3 We share our mutual woes,
  Our mutual burdens bear;
And often for each other flows
  The sympathizing tear.

4 When we asunder part,
  It gives us inward pain;
But we shall still be joined in heart,
  And hope to meet again.

211 How Gentle God's Commands!

1 How gentle God's commands!
  How kind his precepts are!
Come, cast your burdens on the Lord,
  And trust his constant care.

2 His bounty will provide,
  His saints securely dwell;
That hand which bears creation up,
  Shall guard his children well.

3 Why should this anxious load
  Press down your weary mind?
Oh, seek your heavenly Father's throne,
  And peace and comfort find!

4 His goodness stands approved,
  Unchanged from day to day;
I'll drop my burden at his feet,
  And bear a song away.

212 Sow in the Morn thy Seed.

1 Sow in the morn thy seed;
  At eve hold not thy hand;
To doubt and fear give thou no heed,
  Broadcast it o'er the land.

2 Thou know'st not which shall thrive,
  The late or early sown;
Grace keeps the precious germ alive,
  When and wherever strown.

3 Thou canst not toil in vain;
  Cold, heat, and moist, and dry,
Shall foster and mature the grain
  For garners in the sky.

4 Then, when the glorious end,
  The day of God, shall come,
The angel reapers shall descend,
  And heaven shout, "Harvest home!"

213 Did Christ o'er Sinners weep.

1 Did Christ o'er sinners weep,
  And shall our cheeks be dry?
Let floods of penitential grief
  Burst forth from every eye.

2 A cloud of witnesses around
  Hold thee in full survey;
Forget the steps already trod,
  And onward urge thy way.

3 'Tis God's all-animating voice
  That calls thee from on high;
'Tis his own hand presents the prize
  To thine aspiring eye

Hamburg. L. M.

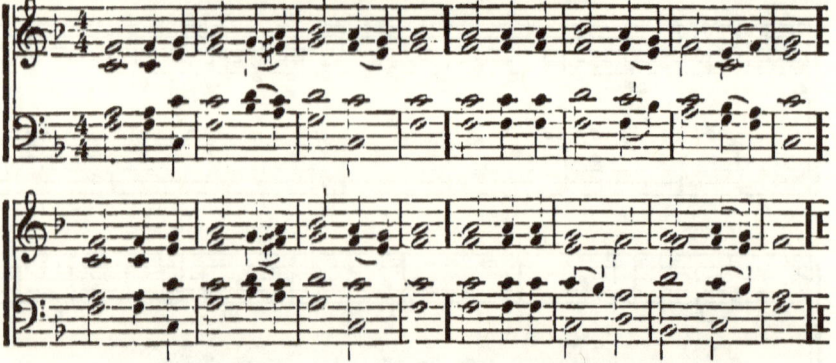

214 **While Life Prolongs.**

1 While life prolongs its precious light,
  Mercy is found, and peace is given,
  But soon, ah! soon, approaching night
  Shall blot out every hope of heaven.

2 While God invites, how blest the day,
  How sweet the Gospel's charming sound;
  Come, sinners, haste, oh, haste away,
  While yet a pardoning God is found.

3 Soon, borne on time's most rapid wing,
  Shall death command you to the grave:
  Before his bar your spirits bring,
  And none be found to hear or save.

4 In that lone land of deep despair,
  No Sabbath's heavenly light shall rise—
  No God regard your bitter prayer,
  No Saviour call you to the skies.

215 **Just as I am.**

1 Just as I am, without one plea,
  But that thy blood was shed for me,
  And that thou bids't me come to thee,
  O Lamb of God, I come! I come!

2 Just as I am, and waiting not
  To rid my soul of one dark blot, [spot,
  To thee, whose blood can cleanse each
  O Lamb of God, I come! I come!

3 Just as I am, though tossed about
  With many a conflict, many a doubt,
  Fightings within and fears without,
  O Lamb of God, I come! I come!

4 Just as I am—poor, wretched, blind;
  Sight, riches, healing of the mind,
  Yea, all I need, in thee to find,
  O Lamb of God, I come! I come!

5 Just as I am—thou wilt receive,
  Wilt welcome, pardon, cleanse, relieve,
  Because thy promise I believe,
  O Lamb of God, I come! I come!

6 Just as I am—thy love unknown
  Hath broken every barrier down;
  Now, to be thine, yea, thine alone,
  O Lamb of God, I come! I come!

216 **Come, Holy Spirit.**

1 Come, Holy Spirit, calm my mind,
  And fit me to approach my God;
  Remove each vain, each worldly thought,
  And lead me to thy blest abode.

2 Hast thou imparted to my soul
  A living spark of holy fire?
  Oh! kindle now the sacred flame,
  Make me to burn with pure desire.

3 A brighter faith and hope impart,
  And let me now my Saviour see;
  Oh! soothe and cheer my burdened heart,
  And bid my spirit rest in thee.

217 **When I Survey.**

1 When I survey the wondrous cross,
  On which the Prince of Glory died,
  My richest gain I count but loss,
  And pour contempt on all my pride.

2 Forbid it, Lord, that I should boast,
  Save in the death of Christ, my God;
  All the vain things that charm me most,
  I sacrifice them to his blood.

3 See, from his head, his hands, his feet,
  Sorrow and love flow mingled down;
  Did e'er such love and sorrow meet,
  Or thorns compose so rich a crown?

4 His dying crimson, like a robe,
  Spreads o'er his body on the tree
  Then am I dead to all the globe,
  And all the globe is dead to me

5 Were the whole realm of nature mine,
  That were a present far too small;
  Love so amazing, so divine,
  Demands my soul, my life, my all.

Rockingham. L. M.

218. Of Him Who Did Salvation Bring.

1. Of him who did salvation bring,
   I could forever think and sing;
   Arise, ye needy,—he'll relieve;
   prise, ye guilty,—he'll forgive.

2. Ask but his grace, and lo, 'tis given;
   Ask, and he turns your hell to heaven:
   Though sin and sorrow wound my soul,
   Jesus, thy balm will make it whole.

3. To shame our sins he blushed in blood;
   He closed his eyes to show us God:
   Let all the world fall down and know
   That none but God such love can show.

4. 'Tis thee I love, for thee alone
   I shed my tears and make my moan;
   Where'er I am, where'er I move,
   I meet the object of my love.

5. Insatiate to this spring I fly;
   I drink, and yet am ever dry;
   Ah! who against thy charms is proof?
   Ah! who that loves, can love enough?

219. So Let Our Lips and Lives Express.

1. So let our lips and lives express
   The holy gospel we profess;
   So let our works and virtues shine
   To prove the doctrine all divine.

2. Thus shall we best proclaim abroad
   The honors of our Saviour God,
   When his salvation reigns within,
   And grace subdues the power of sin.

3. Religion bears our spirits up,
   While we expect that blessed hope,
   The bright appearance of the Lord,
   And faith stands leaning on his word.

220. Another Six Day's Work is Done.

1. Another six days' work is done,
   Another sabbath is begun;
   Return, my soul, enjoy thy rest,
   Improve the day thy God hath blest.

2. Oh that our thoughts and thanks may
   As grateful incense to the skies, [rise
   And draw from heaven that sweet repose,
   Which none but he that feels it knows.

3. This heavenly calm within the breast
   Is the dear pledge of glorious rest,
   Which for the church of God remains,
   The end of cares, the end of pains.

4. In holy duties let the day,
   In holy pleasures pass away;
   How sweet a Sabbath thus to spend,
   In hope of one that ne'er shall end!

221. Thine Earthly Sabbaths.

1. Thine earthly Sabbaths, Lord, we love,
   But there's a nobler rest above;
   To that our longing souls aspire,
   With ardent love and strong desire.

2. In thy blest kingdom we shall be
   From every mortal trouble free;
   No groans shall mingle with the songs
   Which warble from immortal tongues.

3. Oh, long expected day, begin,
   Dawn on this world of woe and sin;
   Fain would we leave this weary road,
   And sleep in death, and rest in God.

222. Doxology.

To God the Father, God the Son,
And God the Spirit, three in one,
Be honor, praise and glory given,
By all on earth and all in heaven.

223. Jesus, Let Thy Pitying Eye

Chas. Wesley. Tune, PENITENCE. W. H. Oakley.

1. Je-sus, let thy pity-ing eye Call back a wand'ring sheep;
False to thee, like Pet-er, I would fain like Pet-er weep.
Let me be by grace restored, On me be all long suff'ring shown;
D.S.—Turn and look up-on me, Lord, And break my heart of stone.

2. Sav-iour, Prince, enthroned a-bove, Re-pentance to im-part,
Give me, through thy dy-ing love, The hum-ble, con-trite heart:
Give what I have long implored, A por-tion of thy grief unknown;

3. For thine own com-passion's sake The gracious won-der show;
Cast my sins be-hind thy back, And wash me white as snow.
Speak the rec-on-cil-ing word, And let thy mer-cy melt me down.

224. Vain, Delusive World.

1 VAIN, delusive world, adieu,
   With all of creature good;
Only Jesus I pursue,
   Who bought me with his blood.
All thy pleasures I forego,
   I trample on thy wealth and pride;
Only Jesus will I know,
   And Jesus crucified.

2 Other knowledge I disdain:
   'Tis all but vanity;
Christ, the Lamb of God, was slain,—
   He tasted death for me;
Me to save from endless woe
   The sin-atoning Victim died;
Only Jesus, etc.

3 Here will I set up my rest;
   My fluctuating heart
From the haven of his breast
   Shall never more depart:
Whither should a sinner go?
   His wounds for me stand open wide;
Only Jesus, etc.

4 Him to know is life and peace,
   And pleasure without end;
This is all my happiness,
   On Jesus to depend:
Daily in his grace to grow,
   And ever in his faith abide:
Only Jesus, etc.

5 Oh, that I could all invite
   This saving truth to prove;
Show the length, the breadth, the height
   And depth of Jesus' love!
Fain I would to sinners show
   The blood by faith alone applied:
Only Jesus, etc. Chas Wesley.

Ariel. C. P. M.

225   O Love Divine.

1 O LOVE divine, how sweet thou art!
  When shall I find my willing heart
    All taken up by thee?
  I thirst, I faint, I die to prove
  The greatness of redeeming love,
    The love of Christ to me.

2 Stronger his love than death or hell!
  Its riches are unsearchable;
    The first-born sons of light
  Desire in vain its depths to see;
  They cannot reach the mystery,
    The length, the breadth, the height.

3 God only knows the love of God;
  O that it now were shed abroad
    In this poor stony heart!
  For love I sigh, for love I pine;
  This only portion, Lord, be mine;
    Be mine this better part.

4 O that I could forever sit
  With Mary at the Master's feet!
    Be this my happy choice;
  My only care, delight, and bliss,
  My joy, my heaven on earth, be this,
    To hear the Bridegroom's voice.

5 O that I could, with favored John,
  Recline my weary head upon
    The dear Redeemer's breast!
  From care, and sin, and sorrow free,
  Give me, O Lord, to find in thee
    My everlasting rest.

226   O could I Speak.

1 O COULD I speak the matchless worth,
  O could I sound the glories forth,
    Which in my Saviour shine,
  I'd soar and touch the heavenly strings,
  And vie with Gabriel while he sings
    In notes almost divine.

2 I'd sing the precious blood he spilt,
  My ransom from the dreadful guilt
    Of sin, and wrath divine;
  I'd sing his glorious righteousness,
  In which all-perfect, heavenly dress
    My soul shall ever shine.

3 I'd sing the characters he bears,
  And all the forms of love he wears,
    Exalted on his throne;
  In loftiest songs of sweetest praise,
  I would to everlasting days
    Make all his glories known.

4 Well, the delightful day will come
  When my dear Lord will bring me home,
  And I shall see his face;
  Then with my Saviour, Brother, Friend,
  A blest eternity I'll spend,
    Triumphant in his grace.

227. Jesus, the Name.

C. WESLEY. Tune, CORONATION. C. M.

1. Jesus! the name high over all, In hell, or earth, or sky;
Angels and men before it fall, And devils fear and fly.

2. Jesus! the name to sinners dear, The name to sinners given;
It scatters all their guilty fear; It turns their hell to heaven.

3 Jesus the prisoner's fetters breaks,
   And bruises Satan's head;
Power into strengthless souls he speaks,
   And life into the dead.

4 O that the world might taste and see
   The riches of his grace!
The arms of love that compass me
   Would all mankind embrace.

5 His only righteousness I show
   His saving truth proclaim:
'Tis all my business here below,
   To cry, "Behold the Lamb!"

6 Happy, if with my latest breath
   I may but gasp his name;
Preach him to all, and cry in death,
   "Behold, behold the Lamb!"

228. Crown Him Lord of All.

C. M.

1 All hail the power of Jesus' name!
   Let angels prostrate fall;
Bring forth the royal diadem,
   And crown him Lord of all.

2 Crown him, ye morning stars of light,
   Who fixed this earthly ball;
Now hail the strength of Israel's might,
   And crown him Lord of all.

3 Ye chosen seed of Israel's race,
   Ye ransomed from the fall,
Hail him who saves you by his grace,
   And crown him Lord of all.

4 Sinners, whose love can ne'er forget
   The wormwood and the gall,
Go, spread your trophies at his feet,
   And crown him Lord of all.

5 Let every kindred, every tribe,
   On this terrestrial ball,
To him all majesty ascribe,
   And crown him Lord of all.

6 O that with yonder sacred throng
   We at his feet may fall!
We'll join the everlasting song,
   And crown him Lord of all.

Antioch. C. M.

229   **O for a thousand tongues.**

1. O FOR a thousand tongues, to sing
My great Redeemer's praise;
The glories of my God and King,
The triumphs of his grace!

2. My gracious Master and my God,
Assist me to proclaim,
To spread through all the earth abroad,
The honors of thy name.

3. Jesus! the name that charms our fears,
That bids our sorrows cease;
'Tis music in the sinner's ears,
'Tis life, and health, and peace.

4. He breaks the power of canceled sin,
He sets the prisoner free;
His blood can make the foulest clean;
His blood availed for me.

5. He speaks, and, listening to his voice,
New life the dead receive;
The mournful, broken hearts rejoice;
The humble poor believe.

6. Hear him, ye deaf; his praise, ye dumb,
Your loosened tongues employ;
Ye blind, behold your Saviour come;
And leap, ye lame, for joy.

230   **Joy to the world!**

1. Joy to the world! the Lord is come;
Let earth receive her King;
Let every heart prepare him room,
And heaven and nature sing.

2. Joy to the world! the Saviour reigns;
Let men their songs employ;
While fields and floods, rocks, hills and plains,
Repeat the sounding joy.

3. No more let sin and sorrow grow,
Nor thorns infest the ground;
He comes to make his blessings flow
Far as the curse is found.

4. He rules the world with truth and grace,
And makes the nations prove
The glories of his righteousness,
And wonders of his love.

231   **The Lord's Prayer.**

1. Our Father which art in heaven, hallowed | be thy | name, || Thy kingdom come, thy will be done in | earth, as-it | is in | heaven.

2. Give us this day our | daily | bread, || And forgive us our trespasses, as we forgive | them that | trespass a- | gainst us.

3. And lead us not into temptation, but deliver | us from | evil; || For thine is the kingdom, and the power and the | glory for- | ever and | ever. || A- | men.

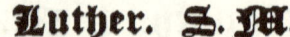

232   I love Thy kingdom

1 I LOVE thy kingdom, Lord,
    The house of thine abode,
The Church our blest Redeemer saved
    With his own precious blood.

2 I love thy Church, O God!
    Her walls before thee stand,
Dear as the apple of thine eye,
    And graven on thy hand.

3 For her my tears shall fall,
    For her my prayers ascend;
To her my cares and toils be given,
    Till toils and cares shall end.

4 Beyond my highest joy
    I prize her heavenly ways,
Her sweet communion, solemn vows,
    Her hymns of love and praise.

5 Sure as thy truth shall last,
    To Zion shall be given
The brightest glories earth can yield,
    And brighter bliss of heaven.

233   Grace!

1 GRACE! 'tis a charming sound,
    Harmonious to the ear;
Heaven with the echo shall resound,
    And all the earth shall hear.

2 Grace first contrived a way
    To save rebellious man;
And all the steps that grace display,
    Which drew the wondrous plan.

3 Grace taught my roving feet
    To tread the heavenly road;
And new supplies each hour I meet,
    While pressing on to God.

4 Grace all the work shall crown
    Through everlasting days;
It lays in heaven the topmost stone,
    And well deserves our praise.

234   Stand up, and bless.

1 STAND up, and bless the Lord,
    Ye people of his choice;
Stand up, and bless the Lord your God,
    With heart, and soul, and voice.

2 Though high above all praise,
    Above all blessing high,
Who would not fear his holy name,
    And laud, and magnify?

3 O for the living flame
    From his own altar brought
To touch our lips, our souls inspire,
    And wing to heaven our thought!

4 God is our strength and song,
    And his salvation ours;
Then be his love in Christ proclaimed
    With all our ransomed powers.

5 Stand up, and bless the Lord;
    The Lord your God adore;
Stand up, and bless his glorious name,
    Henceforth, forevermore.

235   Purity of heart.

1 BLEST are the pure in heart,
    For they shall see our God;
The secret of the Lord is theirs;
    Their soul is his abode.

2 Still to the lowly soul
    He doth himself impart,
And for his temple and his throne
    Selects the pure in heart.

3 Lord, we thy presence seek,
    May ours this blessing be;
O give the pure and lowly heart,—
    A temple meet for thee.

236   Doxology. S. M.

To God, the Father, Son,
    And Spirit, One in Three,
Be glory, as it was, is now,
    And shall forever be.

Boylston. S. M.

LOWELL MASON.

237 And can I yet Delay?

AND can I yet delay
 My little all to give?
To tear my soul from earth away
 For Jesus to receive?

2 Nay, but I yield, I yield;
 I can hold out no more:
I sink, by dying love compelled,
 And own thee conquerer.

3 Though late, I all forsake;
 My friends, my all resign:
Gracious Redeemer, take, oh, take,
 And seal me ever thine.

4 Come, and possess me whole,
 Nor hence again remove;
Settle and fix my wavering soul
 With all thy weight of love.

238 A Charge to Keep I Have.

A CHARGE to keep I have,
 A God to glorify;
A never-dying soul to save,
 And fit it for the sky.

2 To serve the present age,
 My calling to fulfill,—
Oh, may it all my powers engage
 To do my Master's will.

3 Arm me with jealous care,
 As in thy sight to live;
And oh, thy servant, Lord, prepare,
 A strict account to give.

4 Help me to watch and pray,
 And on thyself rely,
Assured, if I my trust betray,
 I shall forever die.

Laban. S. M.

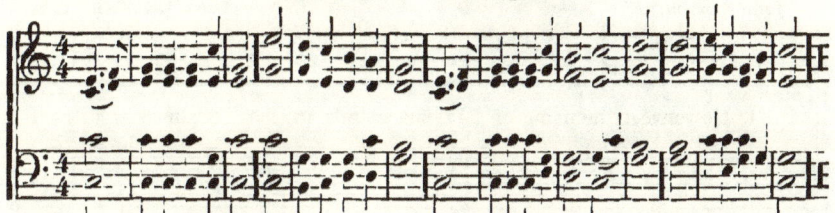

239 Come, Ye that Love the Lord.

COME, ye that love the Lord,
 And let your joys be known;
Join in a song with sweet accord,
 While ye surround his throne.

2 Let those refuse to sing
 Who never knew our God,
But servants of the heavenly King
 May speak their joys abroad.

3 The men of grace have found
 Glory begun below;
Celestial fruit on earthly ground
 From faith and hope may grow:

4 Then let our songs abound,
 And every tear be dry;
We're marching through Immanuel's
 To fairer worlds on high. [ground,

240 My Soul, be on Thy Guard.

MY soul, be on thy guard,
 Ten thousand foes arise,
And hosts of sin are pressing hard
 To draw thee from the skies.

2 Oh, watch, and fight, and pray,
 The battle ne'er give o'er,
Renew it boldly every day,
 And help divine implore.

3 Ne'er think the victory won,
 Nor once at ease sit down;
Thine arduous work will not be done
 Till thou hast got the crown.

4 Fight on, my soul, till death
 Shall bring thee to thy God:
He'll take thee, at thy parting breath,
 Up to his blest abode.

241. When all Thy Mercies.

JOSEPH ADDISON. Tune, MANOAH. C.M.

1. When all thy mer-cies, O my God, My ris-ing soul sur-veys,
Transport-ed with the view, I'm lost In won-der, love, and praise.

2. Through hidden dangers, toils, and deaths, It gently cleared my way;
And through the pleasing snares of vice, More to be feared than they.

3 Through every period of my life
   Thy goodness I'll pursue;
And after death, in distant worlds,
   The pleasing theme renew.

4 Through all eternity to thee
   A grateful song I'll raise;
But oh, eternity's too short
   To utter all thy praise.

242. How Sweet the Name.

JOHN NEWTON. Tune, DOWNS. C.M.

1. How sweet the name of Je-sus sounds In a be-liev-er's ear!
It soothes his sor-rows, heals his wounds, And drives away his fear.

2 It makes the wounded spirit whole,
   And calms the troubled breast;
'Tis manna to the hungry soul,
   And to the weary, rest.

3 Dear name! the rock on which I build,
   My shield and hiding-place;
My never-failing treasure, filled
   With boundless stores of grace!

4 Jesus, my Shepherd, Saviour, Friend,
   My Prophet, Priest, and King,
My Lord, my Life, my Way, my End,
   Accept the praise I bring!

5 I would thy boundless love proclaim
   With every fleeting breath;
So shall the music of thy name
   Refresh my soul in death,

Arlington. C. M.

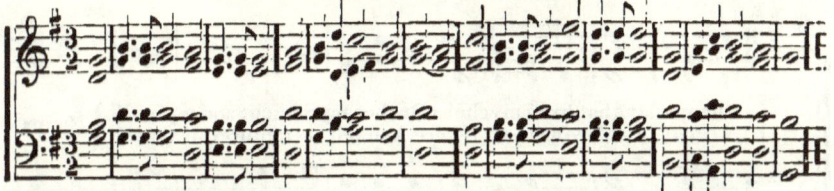

243   *What Glory Gilds.*

WHAT glory gilds the sacred page!
  Majestic, like the sun,
It gives a light to every age;
  It gives, but borrows none.

2 The power that gave it still supplies
  The gracious light and heat;
Its truths upon the nations rise:
  They rise, but never set.

3 Lord, everlasting thanks be thine
  For such a bright display,
As makes a world of darkness shine
  With beams of heavenly day.

4 My soul rejoices to pursue
  The steps of him I love,
Till glory breaks upon my view
  In brighter worlds above.

244   *Am I a Soldier of the Cross?*

AM I a soldier of the cross,
  A follower of the Lamb,
And shall I fear to own his cause,
  Or blush to speak his name?

2 Must I be carried to the skies
  On flowery beds of ease,
While others fight to win the prize,
  And sail through bloody seas?

3 Are there no foes for me to face
  Must I not stem the flood?
Is this vile world a friend to grace,
  To help me on to God?

4 Sure I must fight if I would reign—
  Increase my courage, Lord:
I'll bear the toil, endure the pain,
  Supported by thy word.

Varina. C. M. D.

Geo. F. Root.

245   *How Happy every Child of Grace.*

How happy every child of grace,
  Who knows his sins forgiven!
"This earth," he cries, "is not my place,
  I seek my place in heaven,—
A country far from mortal sight;
  Yet oh, by faith I see
The land of rest, the saints' delight,
  The heaven prepared for me."

2 O what a blessed hope is ours!
  While here on earth we stay,
We more than taste the heavenly powers,
  And antedate that day;
We feel the resurrection near,
  Our life in Christ concealed,
And with his glorious presence here
  Our earthen vessels filled.

3 O would he more of heaven bestow,
  And let the vessels break,
And let our ransomed spirits go
  To grasp the God we seek;
In rapturous awe on him to gaze,
  Who bought the sight for me;
And shout and wonder at his grace,
  Through all eternity.

246. Happy Day.

P. Doddridge. — English Melody.

1. O happy day, that fixed my choice On thee, my Saviour and my God!
   Well may this glowing heart rejoice, And tell its raptures all abroad.
   Happy day, happy day, When Jesus washed my sins away!
   He taught me how to watch and pray, And live rejoicing ev'ry day.

2 O happy bond, that seals my vows
  To him who merits all my love!
  Let cheerful anthems fill his house,
  While to that sacred shrine I move.

3 'Tis done! the great transaction's done!
  I am my Lord's, and he is mine:
  He drew me, and I followed on,
  Charmed to confess that voice divine.

4 Now rest, my long-divided heart;
  Fixed on this blissful center, rest;
  Nor ever from thy Lord depart;
  With him of every good possessed.

5 High heav'n that heard the solemn vow,
  That vow renewed shall daily hear,
  Till in life's latest hour I bow,
  And bless in death a bond so dear.

247. He Came to Save Me.

H E. Blair. — Wm. J. Kirkpatrick.

1. When Jesus laid his crown aside, He came to save me;
   When on the cross he bled and died, . . . He came to save me.
2. In my poor heart he deigns to dwell, He came to save me;
   Oh, praise his name, I know it well, . . . He came to save me.

REFRAIN.
I'm so glad, I'm so glad, I'm so glad that Jesus came, And grace is free,
He . . . came to save me.

3 With gentle hand he leads me still,
  He came to save me;
  And trusting him I fear no ill,
  He came to save me.

4 To him my faith with rapture clings,
  He came to save me;
  To him my heart looks up and sings,
  He came to save me.

Copyright, 1885, by Wm. J. Kirkpatrick.

250. I'll Live for Him.

C. R. Dunbar.

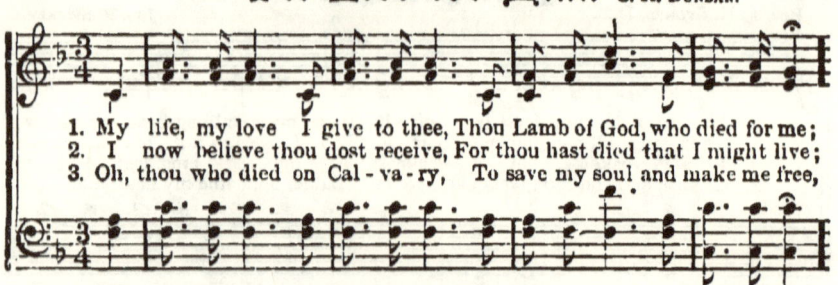

1. My life, my love I give to thee, Thou Lamb of God, who died for me;
2. I now believe thou dost receive, For thou hast died that I might live;
3. Oh, thou who died on Cal-va-ry, To save my soul and make me free,

Cho.—I'll live for him who died for me, How happy then my life shall be!

Oh, may I ev-er faith-ful be, My Sav-iour and my God!
And now henceforth I'll trust in thee, My Sav-iour and my God!
I con-se-crate my life to thee, My Sav-iour and my God!

I'll live for him who died for me, My Sav-iour and my God!

Copyright of R. L. Hudson, used by per.

251. He is Calling.

Arr. by S. J. Vail.

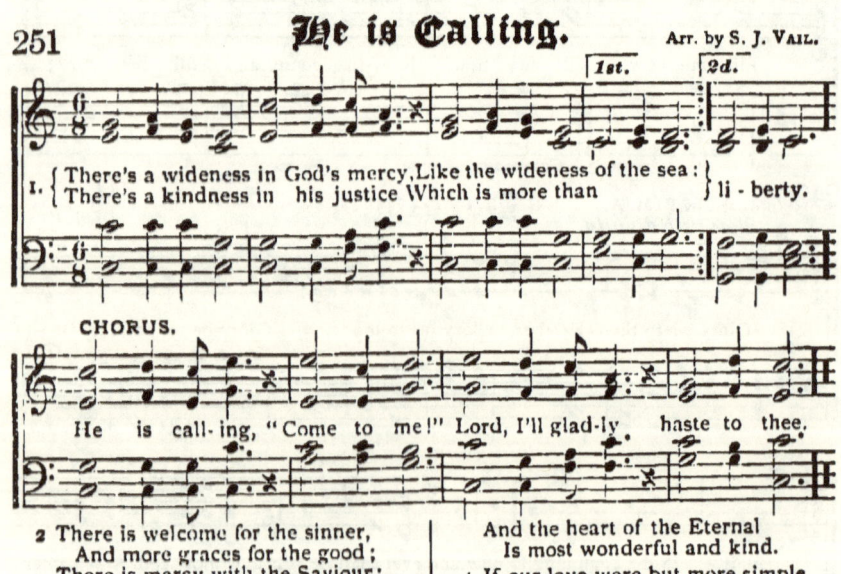

1. { There's a wideness in God's mercy, Like the wideness of the sea:
     There's a kindness in his justice Which is more than } li-ber-ty.

CHORUS.

He is call-ing, "Come to me!" Lord, I'll glad-ly haste to thee.

2 There is welcome for the sinner,
  And more graces for the good;
  There is mercy with the Saviour;
  There is healing in his blood.

3 For the love of God is broader
  Than the measure of man's mind;

And the heart of the Eternal
Is most wonderful and kind.

4 If our love were but more simple,
  We should take him at his word;
  And our lives would be all sunshine
  In the sweetness of our Lord.

252. I'm Going Home to Die no More.

WM. HUNTER, D. D.   Arranged by Rev. WM. MCDONALD.

1. My heav'nly home is bright and fair; Nor pain, nor death can enter there:
Its glitt'ring tow'rs the sun outshine; That heav'nly mansion shall be mine.

CHO. I'm go-ing home, I'm go-ing home, I'm going home to die no more!
To die no more, to die no more, I'm going home to die no more!

2 My Father's house is built on high,
Far, far above the starry sky:
When from this earthly prison free,
That heavenly mansion mine shall be.

3 While here a stranger far from home,
Affliction's waves may round me foam;
Although like Lazarus, sick and poor,
My heavenly mansion is secure.

4 Let others seek a home below,
Which flames devour, or waves o'erflow;
Be mine a happier lot to own,
A heavenly mansion near the throne.

5 Then fail this earth, let stars decline
And sun and moon refuse to shine,
All nature sink and cease to be,
That heavenly mansion stands for me.

253. In the Cross of Christ.

JOHN BOWRING.   Tune, WELLESLEY.   L. S. TOURJEE. By per.

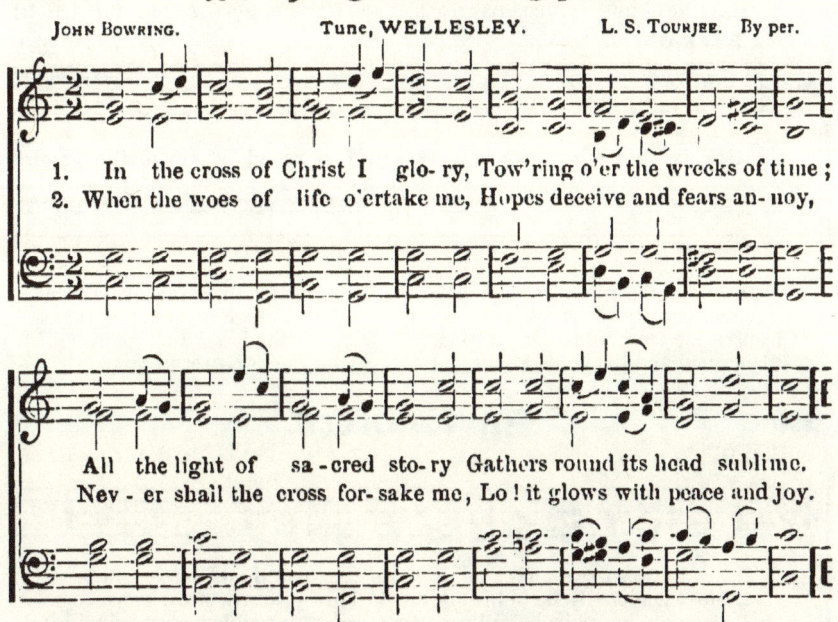

1. In the cross of Christ I glo-ry, Tow'ring o'er the wrecks of time;
All the light of sa-cred sto-ry Gathers round its head sublime.

2. When the woes of life o'ertake me, Hopes deceive and fears an-noy,
Nev-er shall the cross for-sake me, Lo! it glows with peace and joy.

3 When the sun of bliss is beaming
Light and love upon my way,
From the cross the radiance streaming
Adds new lustre to the day.

4 Bane and blessing, pain and pleasure
By the cross are sanctified;
Peace is there that knows no measure,
Joys that through all time abide.

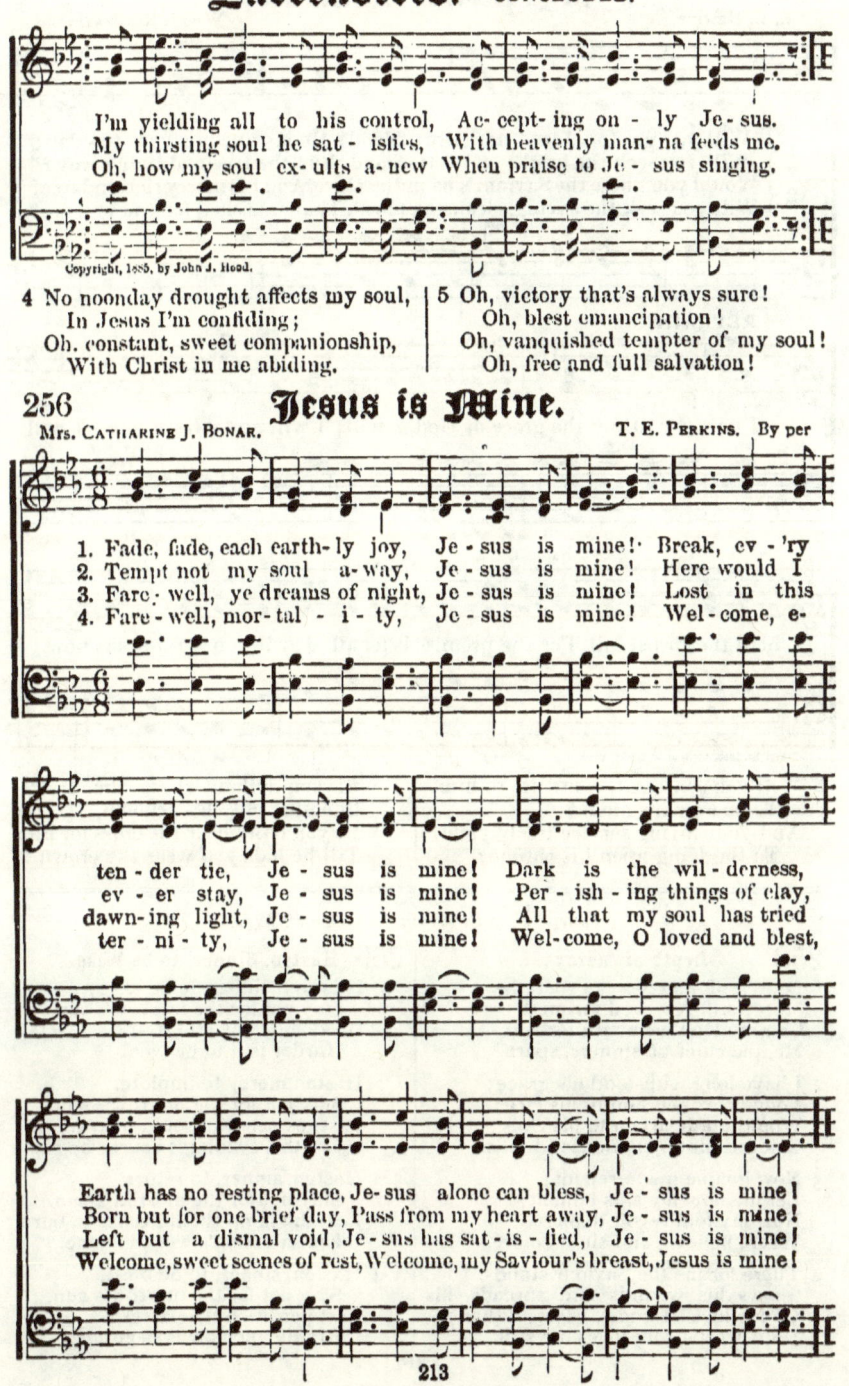

257. By Grace I Will.

E. E. Hewitt. — Wm. J. Kirkpatrick.

1. Will you go to Jesus now, dear friend? He is calling you to-day;
Will you seek the bright and better land, By "the true and living way?"

2. Would you know the Saviour's boundless love, And his mercy rich and free?
Will you seek the saving, cleansing blood, That was shed for you and me?

REFRAIN.
I will, I will! by the grace of God, I will; I will go to Jesus now; I will heed the gospel call, For the promise is for all; I will go to Jesus now.

Copyright, 1888, by Wm. J. Kirkpatrick.

3 Will you consecrate your life to him,
To be ever his alone?
And your loving service freely yield,
To the King upon his throne?

4 Will you follow where the Master leads,
Choosing only his renown,
Will you daily bear the cross for him
Till he bids you wear the crown?

Tune, "Pleyel's Hymn," on opposite page.

258. Depth of Mercy!

Depth of mercy! can there be
Mercy still reserved for me?
Can my God his wrath forbear,—
Me, the chief of sinners, spare?

2 I have long withstood his grace;
Long provoked him to his face;
Would not hearken to his calls;
Grieved him by a thousand falls.

3 Now incline me to repent;
Let me now my sins lament;
Now my foul revolt deplore,
Weep, believe, and sin no more.

4 There for me the Saviour stands,
Shows his wounds and spreads his hands;
God is love! I know, I feel;
Jesus weeps, and loves me still.

259. Hasten, Sinner, to be Wise.

Hasten, sinner, to be wise;
Stay not for the morrow's sun:
Wisdom if you still despise,
Harder is it to be won.

2 Hasten mercy to implore,
Stay not for the morrow's sun,
Lest thy season should be o'er,
Ere this evening's course be run.

3 Hasten, sinner, to return,
Stay not for the morrow's sun,
Lest thy lamp should cease to burn
Ere salvation's work is done.

4 Hasten, sinner, to be blest,
Stay not for the morrow's sun,
Lest perdition thee arrest,
Ere the morrow is begun.

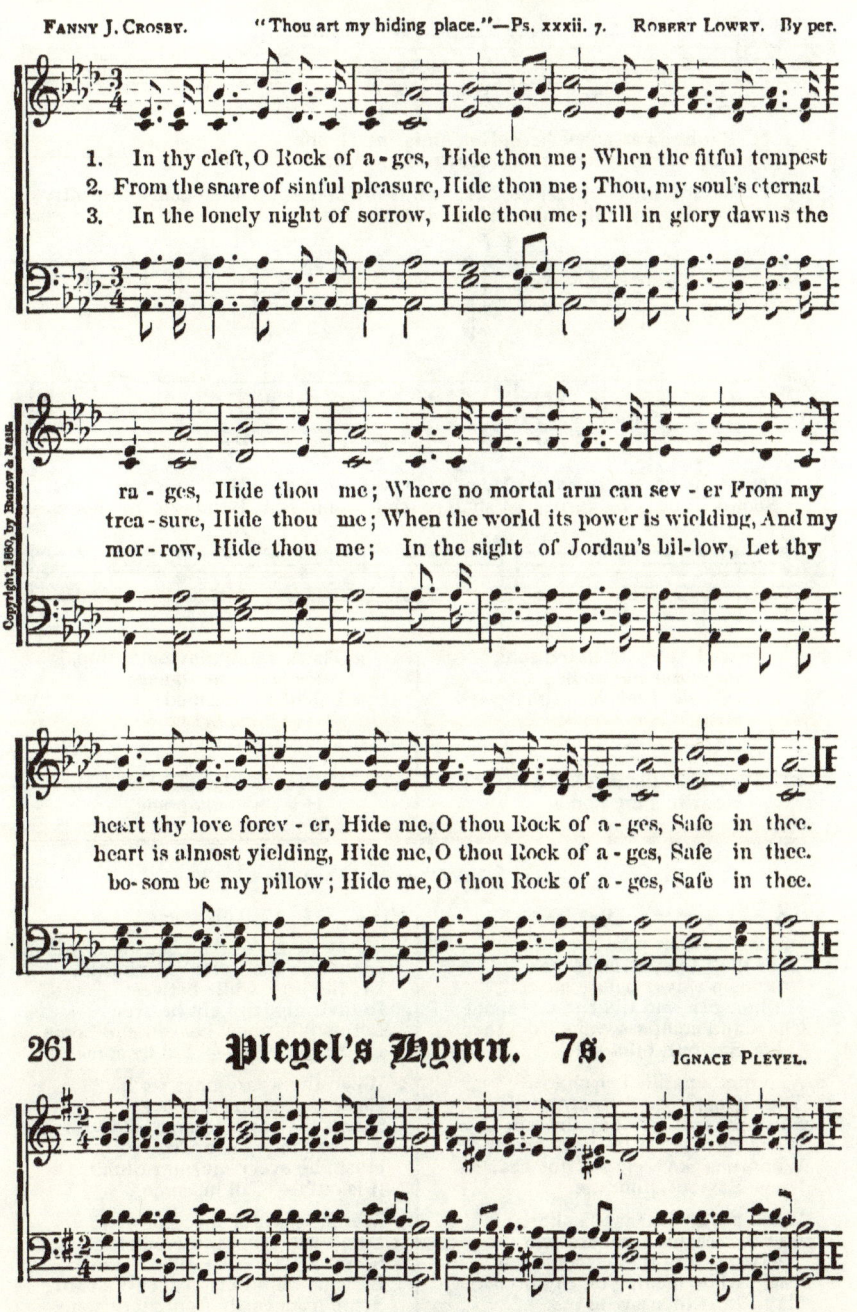

262 Heaven is My Home.

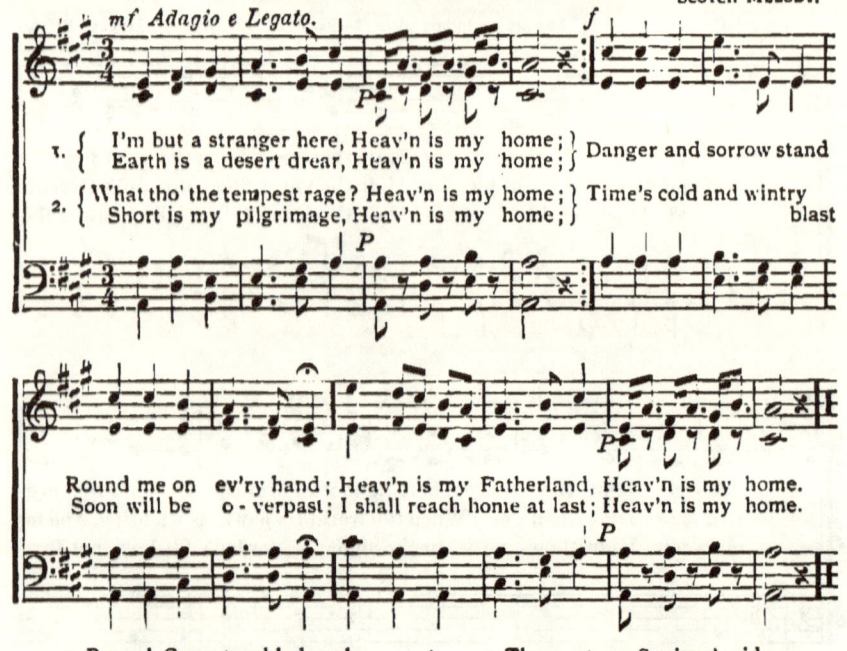

3 Peace! O my troubled soul,
Heav'n is my home;
I soon shall reach the goal;
Heav'n is my home;
Swiftly the race I'll run,
Yield up my crown to none;
Forward! the prize is won;
Heav'n is my home.

4 There, at my Saviour's side,
Heav'n is my home;
I shall be glorified;
Heav'n is my home;
There are the good and blest,
Those I loved most and best,
There, too, I soon shall rest,
Heav'n is my home.

Tune, "Gould," on opposite page.

263 Saviour, Pilot Me.

Jesus, Saviour, pilot me
Over life's tempestuous sea;
Unknown waves before me roll,
Hiding rock and treacherous shoal;
Chart and compass came from thee:
Jesus, Saviour, pilot me.

2 As a mother stills her child
Thou canst hush the ocean wild;
Boisterous waves obey thy will
When thou say'st to them "Be still,"
Wondrous Sovereign of the sea,
Jesus, Saviour, pilot me.

3 When at last I near the shore,
And the fearful breakers roar
'Twixt me and the peaceful rest,
Then, while leaning on thy breast,
May I hear thee say to me,
"Fear not, I will pilot thee."

264 Till He Come.

"Till he come!" oh, let the words
Linger on the trembling chords;
Let the little while between
In their golden light be seen;
Let us think how heaven and home
Lie beyond that—"Till he come."

2 When the weary ones we love
Enter on their rest above,
Seems the earth so poor and vast,
All our life-joy overcast?
Hush, be every murmur dumb;
It is only—"Till he come."

3 See, the feast of love is spread,
Drink the wine, and break the bread;
Sweet memorials,—till the Lord
Calls us round his heavenly board;
Some from earth, from glory some,
Severed only—"Till he come."

265. I Shall be Satisfied.

Bonar.   Moderato.   Rev. T. C. Neal.

1. When I shall wake in that fair morn of morns, Af - ter whose dawning never night returns, And with whose glory day eternal burns, I shall be satis- fied.
2. When I shall see thy glo - ry face to face, When in thine arms thou wilt thy child embrace, When thou shalt open all thy stores of grace, I shall be satisfied.
3. When I shall meet with those that I have loved, Clasp in my eag - er arms the long removed, And find how faithful thou to me hast proved, I shall be satisfied.
4. When I shall gaze up - on the face of him Who for me died, with eye no longer dim, And praise him with the everlasting hymn, I shall be satisfied.

CHORUS.   rit.

I shall be satisfied, I shall be satisfied, I shall be sat-is-fied, By and by.

266. Gould. 7s, 6 lines.

J. E. Gould.

267. I'll be There.

ISAAAC WATTS.   Adapted by WM. J. KIRKPATRICK.

1. There is a land of pure delight, Where saints immortal reign;
 In-fi-nite day excludes the night, And pleasures banish pain.
2. There everlasting spring abides, And never-with'ring flowers;
 Death, like a narrow sea, divides This heavenly land from ours.

REFRAIN.
I'll be there, I'll be there, When the first trumpet sounds I'll be there,
I'll be there, I'll be there, I'll be there, When the first trumpet sounds I'll be there.

3 Sweet fields beyond the swelling flood
   Stand dressed in living green;
So to the Jews old Canaan stood,
   While Jordan rolled between.

4 Could we but climb where Moses stood,
   And view the landscape o'er, [flood
Not Jordan's stream, nor death's cold
   Should fright us from the shore.

Copyright, 1887, by WM. J. KIRKPATRICK.

268. Lord, Dismiss Us.
Tune, "Greenville," opposite page.

LORD, dismiss us with thy blessing,
   Fill our hearts with joy and peace;
Let us each, thy love possessing,
   Triumph in redeeming grace:
     Oh, refresh us,
   Traveling through this wilderness.

2 Thanks we give, and adoration,
   For thy gospel's joyful sound;
May the fruits of thy salvation
   In our hearts and lives abound;
     May thy presence
   With us evermore be found.

3 So, whene'er the signal's given
   Us from earth to call away,
Borne on angel's wings to heaven,
   Glad the summons to obey,
     May we ever
   Reign with Christ in endless day.

269 Come, Ye Sinners.

JOSEPH HART. Tune, GREENVILLE, 8, 7, 4.

Come, ye sinners, poor and needy,
  Weak and wounded, sick and sore;
Jesus ready stands to save you,
  Full of pity, love, and power:
    He is able,
  He is willing: doubt no more.

2 Now, ye needy, come and welcome;
  God's free bounty glorify:
True belief and true repentance,
  Every grace that brings you nigh,
    Without money,
  Come to Jesus Christ and buy.

3 Let not conscience make you linger,
  Nor of fitness fondly dream;
All the fitness he requireth
  Is to feel your need of him,
    This he gives you;
  'Tis the Spirit's glimmering beam.

4 Come, ye weary, heavy-laden,
  Bruised and mangled by the fall;
If you tarry till you're better,
  You will never come at all;
    Not the righteous—
  Sinners Jesus came to call.

5 Agonizing in the garden,
  Your Redeemer prostrate lies;
On the bloody tree behold him!
  Hear him cry, before he dies,
    "It is finished!"
  Sinners, will not this suffice?

6 Lo! the incarnate God, ascending,
  Pleads the merit of his blood:
Venture on him, venture freely;
  Let no other trust intrude:
    None but Jesus
  Can do helpless sinners good.

270 Turn to the Lord. 8, 7.

JEREMIAH INGALLS.

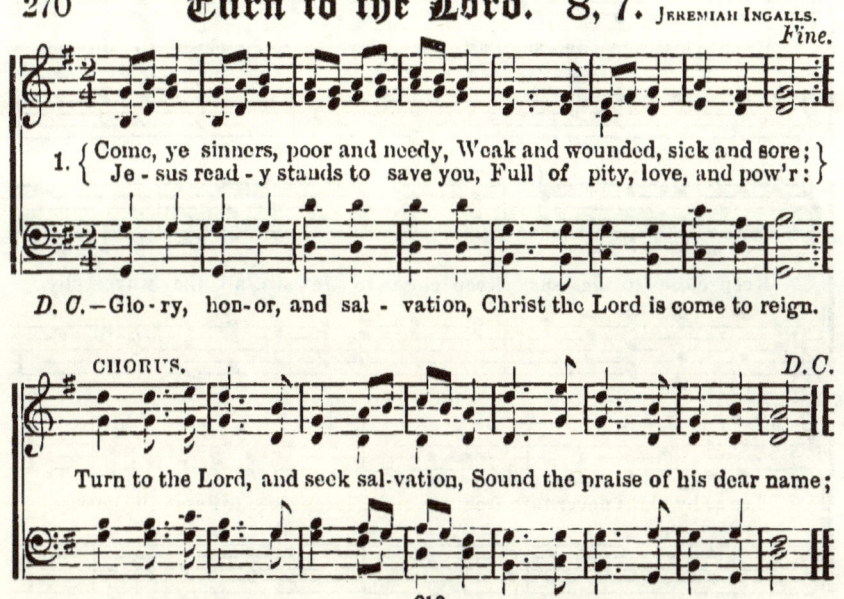

TOPICAL INDEX.

ACCEPTANCE, 22, 96, 109, 183, 257.
ASPIRATION, 71, 103, 197, 209, 224, 225, 245.
ASSURANCE, 6, 31, 47, 55, 70, 130, 149, 167, 170, 171, 256.
ATONEMENT, 65, 75, 119.
AWAKENING, 36, 98, 104, 214, 238, 258, 259.
BIBLE, 243.
CHRISTIAN ACTIVITY, 10, 14, 17, 34, 37, 39, 45, 46, 51, 52, 66, 67, 73, 74, 76, 89, 100, 103, 108, 112, 114, 115, 121, 124, 136, 145, 159, 169, 174, 191, 208, 212, 240, 244.
CHURCH, 210, 232.
CLOSING, 18, 133, 268.
CONFIDENCE, 8, 30, 50, 80, 116, 120, 123, 126, 144, 147, 168, 253.
CONSECRATION, 7, 48, 122, 125, 151, 174, 191, 217, 224, 237, 250, 255.
DEVOTION, 12, 129, 140, 155, 225, 260.
ENCOURAGEMENT, 102, 128, 194, 213, 264.
FAITH, 17, 38, 61, 157, 195, 202.
FELLOWSHIP, 160, 210.
GUIDANCE, 148, 162, 263.
HEAVEN, 4, 13, 19, 20, 32, 43, 60, 62, 78, 86, 90, 102, 132, 146, 154, 156, 187, 252, 262, 265, 267.
HOLY SPIRIT, 40, 88, 199, 216, 248.
INVITATION, 5, 21, 23, 49, 54, 56, 63, 72, 78, 81, 94, 97, 98, 101, 134, 135, 148, 152, 161, 182, 185, 186, 200, 206, 207, 211, 251, 257, 269, 270.
JESUS, 24, 25, 35, 57, 58, 65, 95, 99, 107, 119, 138, 142, 165, 172, 186, 196, 226, 227, 228, 242, 256, 271.
LIVING, 51, 219.
MISCELLANEOUS, 62, 93, 160, 177.
MISSIONARY, 33, 79, 103, 110, 112, 203.
OPENING, 88.
PENITENCE, 29, 63, 89, 189, 193, 215, 223, 257.
PERSEVERANCE, 240.
PRAISE, 1, 92, 111, 166, 198, 201, 218, 226, 228, 229, 230, 234, 241, 249.
PRAYER, 91, 164, 192.
PROMISES, 113, 167.
PURITY, 16, 50, 118, 233.
REFUGE, 12, 70, 83, 116, 140, 149, 180, 196, 260.
REJOICING, 11, 41, 87, 106, 117, 154, 184, 190, 239, 246.
REST, 77, 185, 207.
SABBATH, 220, 221.
SALVATION, 9, 26, 28, 42, 69, 75, 118, 127, 130, 139, 141, 150, 173, 181, 233, 247, 254.
SUPPLICATION, 96, 109, 129, 179, 180, 199, 202, 231.
TESTIMONY, 53, 55, 64, 68, 105, 175, 196, 244, 254.
TRIUMPH, 25.

INDEX.

Titles in CAPITALS; First lines in Roman; Metrical Tunes in *Italics*

	HYMN.		HYMN.		HYMN.
A BLESSING IN PR.	91	Come, contrite one,	82	FULL ASSURANCE,	170
A charge to keep I	238	Come, Holy Spirit, c.	216		
A cry comes over the	112	Come, Holy Spirit, h.	188	GATHERING ONE BY.	187
Alas! and did my	122	Come, sinners, to the g	200	GIVE ME JESUS,	58
A little talk with Je-	164	Come, sinners, to the	57	GLORIOUS AS THE	90
All for Jesus! all for	7	Come to Calvary's	101	GLORIOUS FOUNTAIN,	69
All hail the power of	228	Come unto me when.	185	Glory be to the Fath-	249
All my life long I	130	Come, with all thy	207	GLORY, HE SAVES,	9
All praise to him who	92	Come, ye disconsolate	206	GLORY TO GOD, HAL-	166
ALWAYS ABOUNDING,	159	Come, ye sinners,	269, 270	GLORY TO HIS NAME,	139
Amazing grace! how	173	Come, ye that love	239	Glory to Jesus, he	9
Am I a soldier of the	244	COMING HOME,	22	God loved the world.	42
And can I yet delay?	237	COMING TO-DAY,	54	GOD SO LOVED THE	42
Another six day's	220	COMPANIONSHIP WIT.	142	Go, labor on; spend.	208
Antioch, C. M.,	229	Conquering now, and	6	GOLDEN SHEAVES,	39
Anywhere with Jesus	8	*Coronation, C. M.,*	227	Go tell the story of	121
Are you happy in the	68	Courage, brother, do.	145	GO TELL THE WORLD	33
Ariel, C. P. M.,	225	CROSS AND CROWN,	174	GO TO JESUS,	186
Arlington, C. M.,	243	CROWN HIM LORD	228	*Gould, 7s, 6 lines,*	266
As doves to their win-	70			Go, work in my vine-	10
ASHAMED OF JESUS?	172	DECIDE TO-NIGHT,	98	Grace! 'tis a charm-.	233
A SHELTER IN THE	83	*Dennis, S. M.,*	210	*Greenville, 8, 7, 4,*	269
A SINNER LIKE ME,	53	Depth of mercy! can	258		
As the bird flies home	12	Did Christ o'er sin-	213	*Hamburg, L. M.,*	214
AT THE CROSS,	122	Disciples of Jesus,	79	HAPPY DAY,	246
Awake, my s., stretch	209	DO SOMETHING TO-	100	HARVEST TIME,	52
Awake, my soul, to	201	DO THE RIGHT,	145	Hasten, sinner, to be	259
Away beyond the	78	Down at the cross wh.	139	HEAR AND ANSWER	155
		Downs, C. M.,	242	Hear the shout of tri-	15
BEAUTIFUL ROBES,	156	DOXOLOGY, 222, 236,	249	Hear you not the	148
Be earnest, my broth-	159	Do you hear that gen-	135	HEAVEN IS MY HOME	262
Behold a stranger at.	49			Heirs to the kingdom	33
BEHOLD THE WAY,	137	ENTIRE CONSECRA-.	48	HE IS CALLING,	251
Blessed assurance,	47	EVEN ME,	109	HE CAME TO SAVE	247
BLESSED BE THE N.	92	EVERY NEED SUP-	158	HE'LL MENTION TH..	28
Blest are the pure in.	235			HELP JUST A LITTLE	34
Blest be the tie that.	210	Fade, fade, each	256	Here in thy name we	88
Boyleston, S. M.,	237	Fading away like the	46	HE'S MIGHTY TO SAVE	141
Brother for Christ's.	34	FAIR PORTALS,	86	He that dwelleth in.	116
BROTHER, WILL YOU	78	FAITHFUL GUIDE,	199	HIDE THOU ME,	260
BROUGHT BACK,	63	Father, I stretch my.	195	HIM THAT COMETH	5
BY GRACE I WILL,	257	FED UPON THE FIN-.	129	Holy, holy, holy,	1
		FILL ME NOW,	248	Holy Spirit, faithful.	199
CALVARY,	65	FLASH THE TOP-	103	Hover o'er me, Holy	248
Can a boy forget his.	177	FOLLOW ALL THE	191	HOW CAN I KEEP FR.	117
CHRISTIAN REUNION	160	FOLLOW ME,	148	How gentle God's	211
Christmas, C. M.	209	For Christ and the	136	How happy every	170, 245
Church of God, whose	124	Forever here my	123	How restless the soul	63

222

INDEX.

How sweet the name	242			My faith looks up to	202
Hungry, Lord, for	129	Jesus, and shall it ev-	172	MY FATHERLAND,	85
		JESUS FOR ME,	99	MY FATHER'S HOUSE	13
I am praying, blessed	155	Jesus, I come to thee	196	My heavenly home is	252
I AM RESTING IN THE	120	JESUS IS CALLING	56	My life flows on in	117
I am so weak, dear	158	JESUS IS GOOD TO ME	25	My life, my love I	250
I DO BELIEVE,	195	JESUS IS MINE,	256	My soul, be on thy	240
I fled from Egypt's	55	JESUS IS PASSING BY,	82	My soul in sad exile,	149
I gave my life for	74	Jesus is the light, the	169	My soul sings glory	28
I have a song I love,	175	Jesus is waiting his	141		
I have been to Jesus,	176	Jesus, let thy pitying	223	Nearer, my God! to	197
I have heard my Sav-	191	JESUS LIVES,	76	NEVER TO SAY FARE-	133
I have sown the seed,	128	Jesus, lover of my	180		
I have surrendered to	255	Jesus my all to heav-	137	O bless the Lord,	190
I heard the voice of	183	Jesus, my Saviour, is	99	O Christian, awake!	45
I know that heaven	80	JESUS SAVES,	127	O come to Calvary	56
I'LL BE THERE,	267	JESUS SAVES ME,	254	O could I speak the	226
I'LL LIVE FOR HIM,	250	Jesus, Saviour, pilot	263	Of him who did sal-	218
I love my Saviour,	25	Jesus! the name high	227	O for a heart whiter	16
I love thy kingdom,	232	JESUS WILL GIVE YOU	21	O for a thousand	229
I'm but a stranger	262	JESUS WILL MEET	101	O happy day, that	246
I'm far away from my	13	JESUS WILL WELCOME	131	O have you not heard	146
I'M GOING HOME TO	252	Joy to the world! the	230	Oh, bless d fellowship	142
I'm happy, so happy!	30	Just as I am, thine	59	Oh, my heart is	120
I'M IN THE PROMISED	55	Just as I am, without	215	Oh, sing of Jesus,	64
I'M REDEEMED,	64			Oh, the song of the	143
I'm saved! I'm saved	26	KEEP CLOSE TO JESUS	271	Oh, why should we	94
I must have the Sav-	151			O love divine, how	225
In a world so full of	115	Laban, S. M.,	239	O mourner in Zion,	113
In darkness I wan-	144	LEAD ME, SAVIOUR,	162	On Calvary's brow	65
In dreams I hear a	32	LEANING ON JESUS,	168	Once for all the Sav-	75
IN THE BOOK OF LIFE	96	LEANING ON THE EV-	171	One by one, th' bonds	187
In the crimson of the	138	LET THE BLESSED S..	81	One more witness for	105
In the cross of Christ	253	Life wears a different	41	ONLY BELIEVE,	94
In the good old way	19	LIGHT WILL GREET	102	ONLY REMEMBERED,	46
IN THE SHADOW OF	119	Listen to the blessed	5	On the desert moun	111
IN THE SHAD. OF THY	116	LIVING FOR JESUS,	114	On the happy, golden	60
In thy book, where	96	LOOK AND LIVE,	97	ON THE SHOALS,	112
In thy cleft, O Rock	260	LOOK UP, LIFT UP,	14	ON THE WAY,	190
Into the fountain of	118	Look up to Jesus,	14	Our Father which	231
I SHALL BE SATIS-	265	Lord, dismiss us with	268	Our friends on earth	18
IS MY NAME WRITTEN	93	Lord, I care not for	93	Out in the breakers	37
Is thy trembling	102	Lord, I hear of show-	109	Out on the desert	54
I thirst, thou wound-	71	LORD, I'M COMING H.	29	Out to sea midst	103
IT JUST SUITS ME,	31	LOVING KINDNESS,	201	Over the river they	131
IT WILL NEVER GROW	146	Luther, S. M.,	232		
I've a message from	97			Pass me not, O gen-	193
I'VE BEEN WASHED	176	Make me a worker	67	Penitence, 7, 6,	223
I've heard of streets	4	Manoah, C. M.,	241	PLENTY TO DO,	10
I've wandered far a-	29	MARCHING ON,	11	Pleyel's Hymn, 7s,	261
I want to be a work-	66	MEET ME THERE,	60	PRAISE, PRAISE HIS	111
I was once far away	53	Mighty army of the	76	Prayer is the key,	192
I WILL GIVE YOU REST	185	Missionary C., L. M.	208	Precious Saviour,	254
I will go, I cannot	89	More about Jesus	35	PURITY OF HEART,	235
I WILL SHOUT HIS	154	MORE FAITH IN JE-	157	PURITY WHITER TH..	118
I WILL TRUST IN THE	123	More like Jesus,	163	PUT MY NAME ON	108
I wish that I had nev-	189	Must Jesus bear the	174		

223

Receive me as I am, 59	The coming of his . 138	*Varina, C. M. D.*, . 245
Rest in Jesus, . . 207	The everlas. arms, 147	Victory thro' Je- . 15
Rest, weary heart, . 77	The everlas. hymn, 1	Victory through . 6
Revive us again, . 198	The golden key, . 192	
Rockingham. L. M., . 218	The gospel feast, . 200	
Rock in the desert, . 95	The haven of rest 149	Waiting for the . 128
Rock of ages, cleft . 179	The joyful sound, . 181	We are never, never . 166
	The lights of home 62	We are sailing o'er 184
Safe in the glory-. 19	The Lord's our Rock 83	We are singing on . 87
Salvation! O the joy- 181	The Lord's prayer 231	Weary with walking. 168
Satisfied, . . 130	The morning light is 203	*Webb*, 7, 6, . . 203
Saved to the utter- . 150	There is a fountain . 69	We have an anchor 165
Save one, . . . 37	There is a land of . 267	We have wandered . 22
Saviour, happy would 61	There is a place where 85	We have heard a joy- 127
Saviour, lead me, . 162	There is peace in my 126	We journey to the . 133
Saviour, pilot me, . 263	There is rest, sweet . 91	We'll be there . 4
Send out the sunlight 44	There's a beautiful . 84	*Wellesley*, 8, 7, . . 258
Send the light, . 110	There's a call comes. 110	We'll meet again, . 132
Serenely dwell the . 147	There's a crown in . 20	We'll never say . 18
Showers of bless-. 88	There's a hand held . 72	We praise thee, O . 198
Since I found my . 41	There's a hand that's 36	We're a happy pil- . 184
Since I have been . 175	There's a place above 119	We shall walk with . 156
Singing for Jesus, . 107	There's a wideness in 251	We walk by faith, . 38
Softly and tenderly . 23	There's sunshine in . 106	What a fellowship, . 171
So I can wait, . 80	There stands a Rock. 24	What a wonderful ' . 81
Soldiers in the ranks 160	The sands of time . 130	What glory gilds the 243
So let our lips and . 219	The Saviour is my . 50	What shall our r. 36
Some go away from . 98	The Saviour with . 151	What will you do . 104
Some happy day, . 32	The seed I have scat- 52	When all thy mercies 241
Sometimes a light . 194	The Shepherd Jesus, 134	When I shall wake in 265
Sowing in the morn-. 39	The song of the s.. 143	When I survey the . 217
Sow in the morn thy. 212	The stranger at . 49	When Jesus laid his. 247
Standing on the prom- 167	The sure founda- . 24	When the jewels of . 90
Stand up, and bless . 234	The tender voice of . 153	When we walk with 17
Stand up, stand up . 204	The very same Je-. 57	Where shall we go . 140
Steersman, steersman 62	The voice of Jesus, 183	While life prolongs . 214
Step out on the pr. 113	The world is my . 79	While struggling . 157
Stepping in the l.. 51	Thine earthly Sab- . 221	While the years . 115
Still out of Christ, . 152	This I did for thee 74	Who'll enroll his . 108
Striving to do my . 114	Though your sins be. 161	Who stands outside . 81
Sunshine in the . 106	Throw out the life- . 73	Who, who are these . 43
Surrendered, . . 255	Thy Holy Spirit, . 49	Why still unsaved 153
Sweeping through 43	Till he come! oh, let 264	Will you come, will . 21
Swing back for one . 86	To God, the Father, G. 222	Will you go with . 182
	To God, the Father, S. 236	Will your anchor . 165
Take my life, and let 48	Treasures in heav- 20	With our colors wav- 11
Take the world, but. 58	Trust and obey, . 17	Wonderful story of . 27
Tell it out with glad- 68	Trusting Jesus, . 61	Work for the night is 205
Tell the story of . 121	Trying to walk in the 51	Wouldst thou find a . 186
That gentle whis- 135	*Turn to the Lord*, 8, 7, 270	
The beautiful l. . 169	Use me, O my gra- . 125	
The beautiful t me 84		You ask what makes 154
The clear light of 144	Vain, delusive world, 224	You're longing to w. 100

www.ingramcontent.com/pod-product-compliance
Lightning Source LLC
Chambersburg PA
CBHW021845230426
43669CB00008B/1083